Mastering Application Development with Force.com

Design and develop state-of-the-art applications using Force.com's powerful development platform

Kevin J. Poorman

[PACKT] enterprise 88
PUBLISHING
professional expertise distilled

BIRMINGHAM - MUMBAI

Mastering Application Development with Force.com

Copyright © 2016 Packt Publishing

All rights reserved. No part of this book may be reproduced, stored in a retrieval system, or transmitted in any form or by any means, without the prior written permission of the publisher, except in the case of brief quotations embedded in critical articles or reviews.

Every effort has been made in the preparation of this book to ensure the accuracy of the information presented. However, the information contained in this book is sold without warranty, either express or implied. Neither the author, nor Packt Publishing, and its dealers and distributors will be held liable for any damages caused or alleged to be caused directly or indirectly by this book.

Packt Publishing has endeavored to provide trademark information about all of the companies and products mentioned in this book by the appropriate use of capitals. However, Packt Publishing cannot guarantee the accuracy of this information.

First published: January 2016

Production reference: 1200116

Published by Packt Publishing Ltd.
Livery Place
35 Livery Street
Birmingham B3 2PB, UK.

ISBN 978-1-78217-281-9

www.packtpub.com

Credits

Author
Kevin J. Poorman

Reviewers
Rakesh Gupta
Zarna Chintan Naik
Rahul Sharma
Gautam Singh

Commissioning Editor
Rebecca Youe

Acquisition Editor
Sonali Vernekar

Content Development Editor
Shweta Pant

Technical Editor
Pranjali Mistry

Copy Editor
Pranjali Chury

Project Coordinator
Shipra Chawhan

Proofreader
Safis Editing

Indexer
Mariammal Chettiyar

Production Coordinator
Nilesh Mohite

Cover Work
Nilesh Mohite

About the Author

Kevin J. Poorman has been working with the Salesforce1 platform since 2008. He has architected and built a number of applications on the platform for enterprises and fortune 500 companies in the advertising industry. He has been a Force. com MVP for 3 years. He is active in the community as a developer user group leader, and he can also regularly be found blogging at http://www.codefriar. com, on Twitter (@codefriar), and on the #salesforce IRC channel as well as on the Salesforce developer forums and Salesforce stack overflow. He has also created and maintains the ngForce library for writing Angular.js apps on the platform. In 2015, Kevin joined the Salesforce Marketing Cloud as a senior customer success architect helping marketers succeed at mobile marketing. He regularly speaks on mobile development using Salesforce1, the Salesforce Marketing Cloud, Ionic, and RubyMotion.

I'd like to take some time to thank those who helped this book become reality. First and foremost, my wife, Stephanie, who's been instrumental in encouraging me when I got anchored in the morass of writer's block. Also, I'd like to thank Reid Carlberg and Jeff Finken, who have always been more my mentors than bosses. And, I couldn't have done any of this without the support and friendship of the Salesforce MVP community. I am truly blessed to have been able to write this while standing on the shoulders of not just giants, but Titans who have never feared reaching out to help others. Thank you all.

About the Reviewers

Rakesh Gupta is a Salesforce MVP, evangelist, trainer, blogger, and an independent Salesforce consultant. He is from Katihar, Bihar, and he lives in Mumbai. He has been working on the Force.com platform since 2011. Currently, he is working as a Salesforce consultant and is a regular contributor to the Salesforce Success Community. He is the coauthor of *Developing Applications with Salesforce Chatter* and *Salesforce.com Customization Handbook*, Packt Publishing, and he is also a technical reviewer of *Learning Force.com Application Development*, Packt Publishing. He is the author of *Learning Salesforce Visual Workflow*, Packt Publishing. He has written more than 150 articles on Flow and Process Builder to demonstrate its use to minimize the code usage. He is one of the flow experts from the industry. He is very passionate about Force.com and shares information through various channels, including his blog at http://automationchampion.com.

He has trained more than 200 professionals around the globe and handled corporate trainings. He has six certifications in Salesforce. He works on all the aspects of Salesforce and is an expert in data migration, integration, configuration, and customization. He is the leader of the Navi Mumbai and Nashik developer user groups in India. He is also the initiator of the Mumbai Salesforce user group. He organizes meetups at regular intervals for the groups he is part of.

He can be reached at info@automationchampion.com, or you can follow him on Twitter at *@rakeshistom*.

I would like to thank my parents, Kedar Nath Gupta and Madhuri Gupta, my sister, Sarika Gupta, and my friend Meenakshi Kalra for helping me make time for writing blogs and encouraging me. Also, I would like to thank the team at Packt Publishing and the author of this book for giving me this unique opportunity.

Zarna Chintan Naik is a proprietor of YES CRM Consultants, a Salesforce.com consulting company based in Mumbai. YES CRM Consultants is primarily focused on Salesforce.com consulting, administration, and training services for clients based around the globe.

Zarna and her team also have expertise in multiple appexchange products, including Conga Merge, Clicktools, Rollup Helper, and Drawloop.

Zarna herself holds multiple certifications: Salesforce.com Certified Administrator, Developer, and Sales and Service Cloud Consultant. Previously, she worked for one of the leading Salesforce.com partners in the USA. She has also reviewed *Learning Force.com Application Development*, *Packt Publishing*. To know more about Zarna and YES CRM Consultants, log on to www.yescrm.org or visit her LinkedIn profile at https://in.linkedin.com/in/zarnadesai.

I would like to thank my parents, in-laws, husband, sister, friends, and family for their continued support for my work.

Rahul Sharma has been working on the Force.com platform since 2010 and is a certified advanced developer and administrator. He has worked on many applications involving custom development and integration. He is an active super contributor to the Force.com community and Stackexchange. He holds a bachelor's degree in electronic engineering and is based out of Mumbai, India. His areas of interest are JavaScript and mobile development other than Salesforce. He can be reached at about.me/rahuls91221.

Some of the other books he has worked on are *Learning Force.com Application Development* and *Visualforce Developer's Guide*, both by Packt Publishing.

Gautam Singh is a computer science engineer, blogger, online trainer, technical reviewer, and a smiling human being. He is from Patna, Bihar, and he lives in San Jose, California, USA.

He has been working with the Salesforce platform since 2012, and from the very start he has contributed to motivating and training a large number of homo sapiens in Salesforce and its certificates. Recently, he was on the reviewer panel for *Learning Force.com Fundamental*, Packt Publishing.

Currently, he works for Jade Global Inc. as a techno functional consultant. He holds numerous Salesforce certifications, such as Certified Developer [DEV-401], Certified Developer [ADM-201], Certified Advanced Developer [ADM-211], and Sales Cloud Consultant. He is now on course to complete the Salesforce Certified Advanced Developer [DEV-501].

Gautam actively contributes to the Salesforce discussion platform and currently holds the SMARTIE [Trusted Contributor] position on developer boards. You can follow him through his active blog at `http://singhgautam02.blogspot.in/`.

In his spare time, he is a backpacker who explores the beauty and heritage of India. If not with Salesforce, you can find him taking part in marathons or expressing his love for dogs.

You can follow him on Twitter at `@retweetgautam` and he can be found on LinkedIn at `http://www.linkedin.com/pub/gautam-singh/24/657/244`.

www.PacktPub.com

Support files, eBooks, discount offers, and more

For support files and downloads related to your book, please visit www.PacktPub.com.

Did you know that Packt offers eBook versions of every book published, with PDF and ePub files available? You can upgrade to the eBook version at www.PacktPub.com and as a print book customer, you are entitled to a discount on the eBook copy. Get in touch with us at service@packtpub.com for more details.

At www.PacktPub.com, you can also read a collection of free technical articles, sign up for a range of free newsletters and receive exclusive discounts and offers on Packt books and eBooks.

https://www2.packtpub.com/books/subscription/packtlib

Do you need instant solutions to your IT questions? PacktLib is Packt's online digital book library. Here, you can search, access, and read Packt's entire library of books.

Why subscribe?

- Fully searchable across every book published by Packt
- Copy and paste, print, and bookmark content
- On demand and accessible via a web browser

Free access for Packt account holders

If you have an account with Packt at www.PacktPub.com, you can use this to access PacktLib today and view 9 entirely free books. Simply use your login credentials for immediate access.

Instant updates on new Packt books

Get notified! Find out when new books are published by following @PacktEnterprise on Twitter or the *Packt Enterprise* Facebook page.

Table of Contents

Preface

Salesforce.com's platform is one of the most exciting and unique development platforms for business applications. A lot of Salesforce development can be done declaratively without writing code, but to truly master the platform, you'll need to be able to develop not only declaratively, but also with code. Ultimately, you will need to know when to use which toolset—declarative or code.

It is relatively easy, in a world with Salesforce developer forums, Stack Overflow, and user groups, to find others who have faced the same issues you're facing. As a developer, it's likely that you can cobble together a solution from posted solutions. Understanding and tweaking those posts into a solution for your particular problem, however, requires a greater mastery of the platform.

This book is all about mastering the platform; taking your skills as a developer and tuning them for the unique features of the Salesforce platform. We'll discuss the architecture and code and which tool to use for the job. It's going to be awesome. So let's get started…

What this book covers

Chapter 1, A Conceptual Overview of Application Development on the Salesforce1 Platform, is a quick refresher of the Force.com development tools and methodologies. We'll discuss the concepts of classes, triggers, and unit testing that we'll be mastering in the further chapters.

Chapter 2, Architecting Sustainable Triggers Using a Trigger Framework, will dive deep into why you would need a trigger, when you should and should not use a trigger, and how to architect triggers for maintainability. Additionally, we'll dig into trigger frameworks that provide cleaner, more scalable solutions that solve many of the problems that plague traditional trigger development.

Chapter 3, Asynchronous Apex for Fun and Profit, is all about Apex classes that implement the batchable, scheduleable, and queueable interfaces as well as the @future method Annotation.

Chapter 4, Lightning Concepts, discusses the four new features of the Salesforce platform that carry the Lightning moniker. We'll start with Lightning connect and move on to cover process builder, app builder, and lightning components.

Chapter 5, Writing Efficient and Useful Unit Tests, talks about unit testing, which is the single most important activity an application developer has to master. However, writing unit tests is rarely seen as exciting. In this chapter, we'll look at how to write *useful* unit tests that help us maintain our application over time.

Chapter 6, Deploying Your Code, takes you to the next step—you've written and tested your code, now what? This chapter is a tour of the many ways to deploy your application metadata from one org to another. Specifically, we'll cover the Ant migration toolkit, IDE deployment, and Change sets. Additionally, we'll briefly touch on packaging as a means of deploying metadata.

Chapter 7, Using, Extending, and Creating API Integrations, demonstrates how to use the sObject and bulk APIs provided by Salesforce as well as how to create your own custom REST endpoints with Apex. Finally, we'll build out a set of classes to make calling external REST APIs as painless as possible.

Chapter 8, Team Development with the Salesforce1 Platform, discusses and works through the pitfalls of team development in general and the unique solutions available to us on the Salesforce1 Platform.

Chapter 9, My Way – A Prescriptive Discussion of Application Development on Salesforce1, looks at overarching best practices for Architecture and Engineering of applications on the Force.com platform in depth. Specifically, we discuss the nature of keeping things simple, testing things well, naming things intuitively, and writing maintainable code. While the rest of the book has been descriptive of the best practices, this chapter is an opinionated prescription for developing Salesforce1 applications.

What you need for this book

All you need to get the most out of this book is your brain, your computer with a modern web browser, and a free Salesforce developer org. You can sign up for a free developer org at `https://developer.salesforce.com/signup`. Of course other tools can help, but they aren't required. Optional tools include Sublime Text 3 (with the MavensMate plugin), Atom (with the MavensMate plugin), and Intellij (with the Illuminated Cloud plugin). Again, these are all completely optional. In later chapters, we'll discuss some JavaScript-related tools but we'll discuss installing them when we get there.

Who this book is for

This book is for Salesforce developers. The more you know about Apex, the more you'll take away from this book. Hopefully, as you master more and more of the platform, you'll be able to revisit this book and take away more each time. Regardless of how much Apex you know, this book can teach us all something about how to master the platform.

Conventions

In this book, you will find a number of styles of text that distinguish between different kinds of information. Here are some examples of these styles, and an explanation of their meaning.

Code, and code mixed in with text are shown as follows: A block of code is set as follows:

```
public class AccountTriggerHandler extends triggerHandler {
  public override void beforeInsert() {
    AccountLib.sanitizeDataForAccounts(Trigger.new);
    ContactLib.createContacts(Trigger.new);
    OpportunityLib.createOpps(Trigger.new);
  }
}
```

When we wish to draw your attention to a particular part of a code block, the relevant lines or items are set in bold:

```
global void execute(Database.BatchableContext BC, List<Account> scope)
{
  List<Account> toDelete = new List<Account>();
  List<Account> toUpdate = new List<Account>();
  for (Account a : scope) {
    if(a.bad_account__c){
      toDelete.add(a);
    } else {
      toUpdate.add(a);
    }
```

New terms and **important words** are shown in bold. Words that you see on the screen, for example, in menus or dialog boxes, appear in the text like this: "Another tab in the bottom pane is the **Tests** tab."

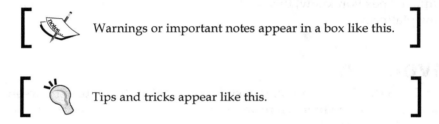

Warnings or important notes appear in a box like this.

Tips and tricks appear like this.

Reader feedback

Feedback from our readers is always welcome. Let us know what you think about this book—what you liked or may have disliked. Reader feedback is important for us to develop titles that you really get the most out of.

To send us general feedback, simply send an e-mail to feedback@packtpub.com, and mention the book title via the subject of your message. If there is a topic that you have expertise in and you are interested in either writing or contributing to a book, see our author guide on www.packtpub.com/authors.

Customer support

Now that you are the proud owner of a Packt book, we have a number of things to help you to get the most from your purchase.

Downloading the example code

You can download the example code files for all Packt books you have purchased from your account at http://www.packtpub.com. If you purchased this book elsewhere, you can visit http://www.packtpub.com/support and register to have the files e-mailed directly to you.

Errata

Although we have taken every care to ensure the accuracy of our content, mistakes do happen. If you find a mistake in one of our books — maybe a mistake in the text or the code — we would be grateful if you would report this to us. By doing so, you can save other readers from frustration and help us improve subsequent versions of this book. If you find any errata, please report them by visiting http://www.packtpub.com/ submit-errata, selecting your book, clicking on the **errata submission form** link, and entering the details of your errata. Once your errata are verified, your submission will be accepted and the errata will be uploaded on our website, or added to any list of existing errata, under the Errata section of that title. Any existing errata can be viewed by selecting your title from http://www.packtpub.com/support.

Piracy

Piracy of copyright material on the Internet is an ongoing problem across all media. At Packt, we take the protection of our copyright and licenses very seriously. If you come across any illegal copies of our works, in any form, on the Internet, please provide us with the location address or website name immediately so that we can pursue a remedy.

Please contact us at copyright@packtpub.com with a link to the suspected pirated material.

We appreciate your help in protecting our authors, and our ability to bring you valuable content.

Questions

You can contact us at questions@packtpub.com if you are having a problem with any aspect of the book, and we will do our best to address it.

1
A Conceptual Overview of Application Development on the Salesforce1 Platform

This chapter will give you a quick refresher on Force.com development tools and methodologies. We'll discuss the concepts of classes, triggers, and unit testing that we'll be mastering in future chapters. Additionally, we'll discuss the tools available for us to write Salesforce1 code. We'll focus on the developer console built into the Salesforce web interface, and you'll learn to use it for daily development tasks. The following topics will be covered in detail in this chapter:

- Cloud computing and development
- Development tools
- Using the developer console

Developing for the cloud

Starting with e-mail, traditional applications for the desktop have been replaced with browser and mobile-based applications. And just like that, cloud computing has become an everyday fact of our lives. Now, you can find applications on the Web running on your browser that handle everything from photo editing and displaying to music streaming services and, of course, running your business. Corresponding to this shift to cloud-based applications, there's been a shift in how we develop software. True, we are no longer writing software on a local machine, publishing it, and having users run it on a local machine; we're now writing software on our local machine and pushing it to the App Store, the cloud, and increasingly connected devices. Salesforce development has always been somewhat different though. The Salesforce1 platform requires developers not only to run their code in the cloud, but to develop it there as well. This has always been the case to some extent, as you can't run an instance of Salesforce on your local computer. The only way to develop new features, to test, or even run your code is to put that code in the Salesforce cloud. Over the years, Salesforce has continually worked to improve this experience, first with the Eclipse-based Force.com IDE, then with the metadata and tooling APIs that facilitate third-party IDE integrations. Now, Salesforce has created the developer console, an in-browser code editor. We will use a developer console throughout the rest of this book to work through exercises, create and edit metadata, and demonstrate various features of Salesforce cloud. Before you can access the developer console, you'll need a developer edition organization. To sign up for a developer org visit the following URL. I highly encourage you to pause and sign up for the development org. Of course, if you already have a developer org, you can reuse it.

When you go to `http://developer.salesforce.com/signup`, the signup page will be displayed, as shown in the following screenshot:

Identifying the development tools

There are three main development tools for building Force.com applications. The first and perhaps the most efficient development tool is the Force.com IDE. The IDE is distributed as a plugin for the venerable Eclipse development environment. If you've done Java development, you will feel at home with this. Additionally, in the past few months, an excellent plugin for the venerable Jetbrains Intellij IDEA IDE has been released. It is called Illuminated Cloud (refer to `http://www.illuminatedcloud.com/` for more information). If you're a fan of the Intellij platform, you'll feel at home with it. The Salesforce community has also established another tool called MavensMate for developing Salesforce1 applications. MavensMate is a set of plugins for the excellent sublime text and the atom text editors. The plugins use the metadata and tooling APIs to provide a rich set of development tools. These tools include logging, anonymous apex execution, and the creation and editing of metadata. Documentation on installation and use of the MavensMate plugin can be found at the MavensMate home page, `http://mavensmate.com/`. The developer console is a relatively new feature to Salesforce. It provides an in-browser tool for developers to create and edit metadata, as well as run tests, execute queries, and generally inquire into the state of your application code. You can access the developer console by clicking on your name in the upper right-hand corner of the screen and selecting developer console, as shown here:

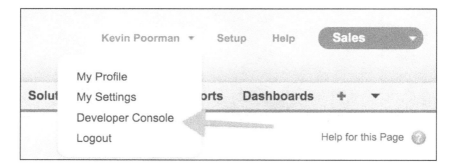

At various points, you'll see text items denoted by the pipe symbol(|), for example, **File | New | Class**.

Let's take a look at the following screenshot of menu instructions for the developer console:

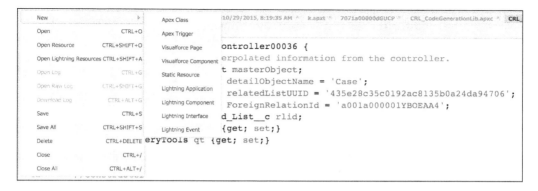

For example, if you click on the **File** menu, followed by the **new** menu item, and finally on the **class** menu item, you'll be given an opportunity to create, name, and create a new Apex class:

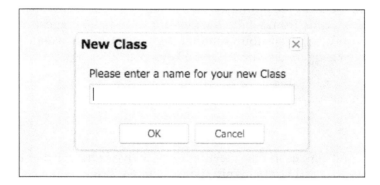

Object-oriented building blocks of Force.com development

The Salesforce1 platform runs the Apex programming language. Like most other contemporary programming languages, Apex is object-oriented. Object-oriented development is focused on the creation of and interaction between objects. Objects are the result of instantiating classes. Classes describe properties and methods that can be interacted with. For instance, you might have a `Box` class, with properties of `height`, `width`, and `depth`. A box object would refer to a specific instance of the class `box`, with it's own values for `height`, `width`, and `depth`. Classes are the basic building blocks of object-oriented development and, therefore, Force.com development. Classes come in many varieties, from Visualforce controllers and controller extensions to inner and wrapper classes and normal classes. We will work with a number of class types throughout the book. Each class type can be created via the developer console using the new class option in the file menu and giving it a name.

While classes are building blocks of object-oriented development in the Salesforce1 ecosystem, there are a couple of other code containers, specifically, triggers and lightning bundles. Aside from where the files are stored, the biggest difference between classes and triggers is found in their first line. Classes use the `class` keyword, whereas triggers use the `Trigger` keyword:

```
//Definition of a class
Public with sharing class myExampleClass {
//Definition of a Trigger
Trigger myExampleTrigger on Account (before insert) {
```

Triggers differ from classes in that they define reflexive behavior that the system takes in response to certain data manipulation actions. Triggers have their own rules and ecosystems, and we will look at them in detail in their own *Chapter 2, Architecting Sustainable Triggers using a Trigger Framework*. Lightning Bundles, on, on the other hand contain more than just code. Lightning bundles also contain other assets like CSS style definitions, icons and documentation.

Learning to master Salesforce1 development

There is an old story about a new developer and a seasoned developer tackling the same problem. The new programmer Googles the problem, and after looking at a few stack exchange posts, pastes together some code and is confident that it works. After all, he thinks, other people have this exact same problem and they helpfully posted their results online. With their help, the new developer can put together a solution. On the other hand, the experienced developer first sits down and writes a test to prove that the problem exists. Only then does the developer write code to try to rectify it. This is one of the key differences between being an application developer and a master application developer. This is equally true for Salesforce1 platform. To truly master the platform, you not only need to know the language, logic, and patterns, but also how to know, objectively, when the code is done. Because of this, we'll be focusing on writing automated tests for our code.

Knowing when your code works is paramount to Apex solutions. However, the Salesforce1 platform provides a number of ways to develop solutions without writing Apex. Almost everything that can be done with the declarative tools can be done with Apex code, but to master the platform, you need to know when to use those declarative tools and when to write Apex.

Using the Salesforce developer console

Our code must live in the Salesforce cloud. Throughout this book, there will be a number of example code segments. Each of these is intended to highlight a technique, pattern, or feature of either Apex or the Salesforce1 platform. While you are free to use MavensMate or the Eclipse Force.com IDE plugin, this book will demonstrate code segments that have been tested in the developer console. Because of this, it's probably a wise idea for us take some time and demonstrate how to use the developer console. Once the window opens, you'll see a two-pane interface generally broken down into a taller pane and a shorter one below it. The menu bar across the top pane gives you access to several development features, while the lower pane gives you access to things such as logs and the query editor. Additionally, you can use this lower pane to access the view state of a visual force page and a number of other features as well. Let's talk about some common use cases for the developer console and walk through how to accomplish them.

Opening and creating metadata

Unless you're working with a brand new developer org that contains no metadata, you can open existing pages, classes, and triggers through the use of the file menu. To open up an existing class choose **File | Open**. You'll see a pop-up window with three panes:

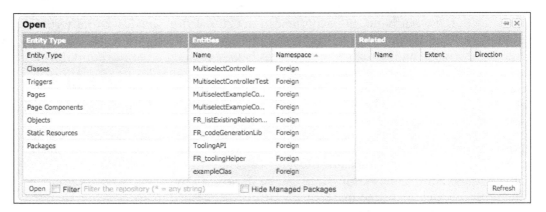

The first pane shows various types of metadata you can open that is **Triggers, Classes, Objects**, and so on. Once you select a metadata type, the middle pane will populate with all of the files of that type. For instance, if you select classes, you'll see all the classes in the org. You can open up any given metadata file by double-clicking on the name in the middle pane. Additionally, other resources, such as lightning bundles and static resource bundles can be opened using the **File** menu option, **Open Resource**. If you've ever used sublime text, this works similarly to the open-anything command. Start typing in the filter modal and it will reduce your selection options helping you find what you're looking for.

Likewise, to create new classes, pages, and triggers use the **New** menu of the Developer console. The new submenu lists all of the various types of metadata you can create in the console, including things such as **Static Resources** and **Visualforce Components**. Ensure that you familiarize yourself with the process of creating new classes, triggers, and Visualforce pages; we will be doing this throughout the book.

Running SOQL and SOSL queries

Across the top of the shorter pane in the developer console is a series of tabs: **Logs, Tests, Checkpoints, Query Editor, View State, Progress**, and **Problems**. One of the most important features of the developer console lies in the ability to run SOQL and SOSL queries directly from it. To open the query editor, click on the **Query Editor** tab. Once opened, you can start typing your query in the lower pane.

Remember that SOQL queries must start with SELECT and SOSL queries must start with FIND when you run a query. After you run a query you'll see the results in the upper pane of the developer console. You can interact with these records by selecting a record and clicking on the command buttons at the bottom of the pane. This allows you to open the record in the Salesforce user interface, or delete the record right there in the developer console, as shown in the following screenshot:

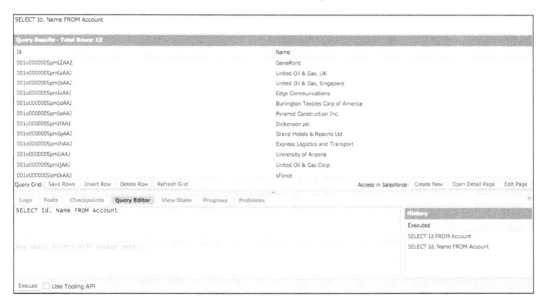

While we're discussing this, let's go ahead and give it a try. Your developer org comes with a certain number of accounts and contacts pre-established. We can run a query right now and experience how the developer console query editor works. Write this query in the query editor of your developer console:

```
Select SELECT Id, name Name from FROM Account;
```

If you're using a new developer org, you'll have between 10 and 12 accounts that are returned as results in the top pane of the developer console. In fact, unless you delete the accounts from your org, this query will always return at least a few records, each column being one of the two fields requested in select clause of the query. Double-click on the **Name** field of the first record. As soon as you do so, you'll find that you can edit the record name right there. However, once you have edited a field on a record, ensure that you hit the **Save record** button at the bottom of the pane. You'll also find buttons to insert a new row, access that record in the Salesforce user interface, and open the records detail page.

Running unit tests

Another tab in the bottom pane is the **Tests** tab. This is where you will run and, otherwise, interact with unit tests. Unit tests are methods of code that we run to execute and test units of live code. We'll talk extensively about unit tests in Chapter 5, *Writing Efficient and Useful Unit Tests*. Unit tests are run asynchronously, meaning they don't run immediately when you fire them up. You'll need to wait a bit while your tests run and the tests tab will show you when they start. As the test run completes, you'll see that the individual suites are completed and the individual tests are underneath them via disclosure triangles. Should you have a failure, you can double-click on the failure to bring up the results of that particular test in the upper portion of the developer console. Here, you can see the tests tab with the test suites and test methods expanded:

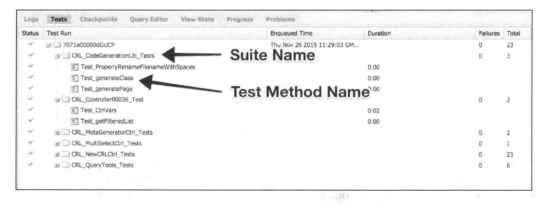

When viewing the **Tests** tab, an additional data pane shows up in the lower-right corner. While the bottom-left pane allows you to view test runs, the bottom-right pane shows you the code coverage for the various classes and triggers in your org:

Overall Code Coverage		»
Class	Percent	Lines
Overall	**0%**	
FR_codeGenerationLib	0%	0/50
FR_listExistingRelationsCtrl	0%	0/1
MultiselectController	0%	0/24
ToolingAPI	0%	0/496

This window shows the overall aggregate code coverage metric that matters when deploying from one org to another and you must have at least 75% of your code covered as measured here. As you can see, I don't have anywhere near the code coverage I need. Double-clicking on a class or trigger listed in this code-coverage pane will open the class and display which lines are covered and which are not. This is an incredibly useful tool for finding testing gaps!

```
2      //this section contains interpolated information from the controller.
3      @testVisible private Account masterObject;
4      @testVisible private String detailObjectName = 'Case';
5      @testVisible private String relatedListUUID = '435e28c35c0192ac8135b0a24da94706';
6      @testVisible private String ForeignRelationId = 'a001a000001YBOEAA4';
7      @testVisible private Related_List__c rlid;
8      public Boolean initialized {get; set;}
9      public CRL_QueryTools qt {get; set;}
10
11     //METHODS
12     //Constructor
13     public CRL_Controller00036(ApexPages.StandardController stdController) {
14         this.initialized = false;
15         this.masterObject = (Account)stdController.getRecord();
16
17     }
18
19     @testVisible
20     private CRL_Controller00036(ApexPages.StandardController stdController, id frid) {
21         this.masterObject = (Account)stdController.getRecord();
22         this.ForeignRelationId = frid;
23         this.qt = new CRL_QueryTools(ForeignRelationId, masterObject.id);
24     }
25
```

Red highlighted lines are NOT covered by tests

Lavender highlighted lines are covered by tests.

Creating and opening Lightning Components

Lightning Components are the building blocks of lightning apps. They're written in JavaScript, Apex, and HTML/CSS; they represent the next evolution of Salesforce application development. If you've enabled Lightning Components in your org, you'll see that the ability to create new Lightning Components is in the same **New** menu list as classes, triggers, and so on. Specifically, you'll see options to create new lightning apps, Lightning Components, lightning interfaces, and lightning events. However, opening lightning resources is slightly different than opening a Visualforce page or an Apex class. Instead of navigating to **File | Open**, you have to use the new open lightning resources menu item in your file. We'll talk more about lightning components in *Chapter 6*, *Deploying Your Code*.

Opening and reading debug logs and adjusting log levels

One of the great benefits of the developer console is that you can read all of the debug logs that come through your org. Debug logs are log files generated by code execution on the platform. Whenever a user navigates to a Visualforce page or a trigger is run, for instance, the platform generates detailed logs about what happened and how long it took, developers can insert data into these logs using the Apex method, `System.debug`(string). By default, only debug logs created when your user has taken action are shown on the **Logs** option. However, you can toggle seeing the debug logs for all users via the **Debug** menu. Once an event that has generated logs has occurred, you'll see them listed under the **Logs** tab, as shown here:

Default sorting is by time, with the newest on top; however, you can sort by the username, application, and so on. More importantly, you are able to sort through them by status. To open the log, simply double-click on it. This will open up in the larger pane of the developer console. Alternatively, if you'd like more of a raw view of the log, you can right-click on it and open **Raw Log**.

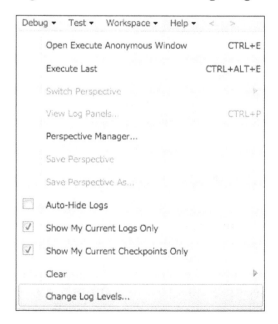

Regardless of how you open the log, the more you deal with them, the more you'll realize they can get to be quite large; sometimes, several megabytes in size. To help with this, the developer console has a way for you to alter the log verbosity. These settings are referred to as the log levels and they provide a fairly fine-grained level of control over how verbose the various system components log. To modify the log levels, click on the **Debug** menu and then select **Change Log Levels**:

Here, you can set the general log levels for a given period of time for database (**DB**) calls, **Callouts**, **Apex Code**, **Validation** (validation rules), **Workflow** (workflow rules), **Profiling** and **Visualforce**, and the **System** itself. Each log type has seven verbosity levels ranging from **ERROR** at the lowest verbosity to **FINEST** at the most verbose. At the most basic, at the least verbose setting of **ERROR**, only true errors are logged. On the other hand, **FINEST** logs the most minute details of the code execution:

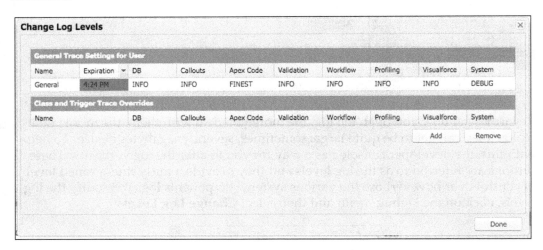

More importantly, you can set per class and per trigger overrides if you want to debug a specific class or trigger. Increasing the logging verbosity for your troublesome class or trigger can help you highlight performance problems as well as logic issues. In general, while writing code, it's good to leave most log types on **INFO** but I set workflow and validation rule logging to error, as workflow and validation rules can log quite a lot.

An anonymous Apex execution

Anonymous Apex is probably one of the most misunderstood and easily overlooked aspects of Force.com development. Anonymous apex allows you to run scripts or snippets of Apex code without compiling it into a class. Functionally, this means that you can run a query and iterate over the results to do a one-off data cleanup script, for example. Alternatively, you can also do functional system tests, such as making callouts and executing code. You can think of this as a little bit like a DOS batch job or a Linux shell script. To access the execute anonymous window, open the developer console and click on the **Debug** menu and then select **Open Execute Anonymous Window**:

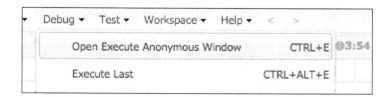

This will open a resizable modal window where you can type the Apex code, as shown in the following screenshot:

```
Enter Apex Code                                                    ▲ ×
1  public Map<String, Schema.SObjectType> gd {get{return Sche
2 ▾ for(String s : gd.keyset()){
3      system.debug('#### ' + s);
4      system.debug(gd.get(s));
5      system.debug('#### END ' + s);
6  }
```

Unlike the `main` class and `trigger editor` you will not receive syntax help, but you will get syntax highlighting. Anonymous apex is not terribly different from a Swiss Army chainsaw. You can do anything you want with it, but if you're not careful, you'll cut your foot off. A mistake can easily delete records or modify them beyond repair. Be careful.

Addressing problems

The last bit of the developer console we need to cover is the **Problems** tab. Should you have a syntax error in any of your code, the **Problems** tab will list them along with the class name and line number:

For instance, if you forget a ; it will list the name of the class, a pretty decent rough estimate of the problematic line number, and what the compilation error is. The **Problems** tab updates asynchronously to other activities. However, it will update a badge style count of errors in the background. Whenever you see a badge icon over the **Problems** tab, you have a syntax error in your code.

Developer console exercises

We'll be using the developer console throughout this book, so it is necessary that you become familiar with it. The following are some exercises to help you familiarize with the consoles development features:

- **Create a class**: Using the developer console, create a new class and give it the name `DevConsoleExample`. Ensure that the class compiles without errors.

- **Run a SOQL query**: Run a SOQL query from the query editor, that finds all the opportunities that are on the closed/won stage.

- **Execute anonymous**: Run the following code block in execute anonymous window:

```
System.assert(1, (1/0), 'should throw an assertion error');
```

- **Log viewing**: Having run that snippet of Apex in the developer console, navigate to the **Logs** tab and open the **raw log** option of its execution. Does the code throw **assertion exception** or **division by 0 exception**?

Summary

In this chapter, we discussed the object-oriented nature of Salesforce's programming language Apex, and dove into how to use the Developer console. Along the way, we discussed a couple of other development tools and hopefully what your appetite for future topics. In our next chapter, we will cover one of the fundamental aspects of Salesforce.com development—Triggers.

2
Architecting Sustainable Triggers Using a Trigger Framework

This chapter starts with a quick refresher on Salesforce triggers. We'll look at the fundamental basics of how they work and when to use them. We'll then look at the concept of a trigger framework and dive deep into the how and why of a particular framework.

In this chapter, we will see the following topics:

- An overview of triggers
- Issues with traditional trigger architecture
- Trigger frameworks
- SFDC-trigger-framework

An overview of triggers

We are all familiar with the strange triangular hammer, which our doctor hits us with in the knee, making our leg kick out involuntarily. The key to reflexes is that they are automatic and programmed deep inside us. So deep, in fact, that at runtime (err, during life), it's a really big deal when our reflexes stop working. Likewise, Salesforce triggers work on a deep system level. Unlike human reflexes, however, we can program Salesforce triggers. Developers get to decide what happens when the reflexes are triggered.

Context is king

Triggers run in a well-defined but developer chosen context. We select the object, the **Data manipulation language (DML)** statement to act on, and even the before and after status of the DML call. DML refers to a set of keywords: insert, update, upsert, delete, and undelete. Triggers are, therefore, one of the most powerful tools in an architect's toolbox. Triggers are phenomenally flexible but with that phenomenal power comes the potential for phenomenal complexity. Because of this, triggers are not without an issue. In fact, their inherent flexibility is their greatest weakness. Salesforce allows you to create multiple triggers on the same object, with the same DML event and the same timeframe. However, Salesforce does not guarantee that your triggers will run in a deterministic order. Because of this, many older orgs with evolutionary changes made over years often run into issues with multiple triggers firing on the same object but without deterministic results.

When discussing triggers, first we need to determine the context in which the trigger will run. The context is made up of three crucial elements:

- The object on which we wish the trigger to fire.
- The DML statement which the trigger should listen for.
- The timeframe in which the trigger will run. Essentially there are two options for this: before and after.

These three bits of information combine to form the trigger context. This information can be composed into a sentence that reads something like account after insert. In this case, account is the object the trigger will act on, insert is the DML statement, and after is our timeframe. Together, this context means our trigger will run after an account is inserted. Context is important because it tells us and the system when the events or trigger will happen. There are many contexts available. We can fire our trigger whenever we insert records, update records, merge records together, undelete records, or upsert records. Combine that with the two time frames before and after, and you end up with a whole host of trigger contexts that are available to us. When I talk about before or after, I'm referring to when the trigger will run. Will the trigger run before the data is inserted? after the insert? before the upsert? or after the delete? Timeframe is almost as important as the DML statement selection since certain features of the trigger framework and data are available to us before or after the DML statement. For instance, we won't have an ID for the record until after we've inserted it. Thus, we can't build logic in our triggers that relies on the records having an ID unless it's an after insert statement, or after the upsert trigger.

Trigger variables

Salesforce provides us with sets of trigger variables. These trigger variables are not available during all contexts. The first set of trigger variables are accessed via `Trigger.new` and `Trigger.old`. Both of these variables are lists containing each of the records that are being passed to the trigger for processing. These are typed, so if we fire trigger on our account, we will be given a list of accounts to process. As you might imagine, `Trigger.old` contains the values of the records prior to the trigger variable of the DML statement that fired this trigger. The `Trigger.new` variable represents what was just saved or what will be saved depending on the time frame of your trigger. For instance, in a before update trigger, the `trigger.new` variable contains the updated values of the records being updated. Conversely, `trigger.old` contains the original, unupdated values of the records being updated. Our second set of trigger variables is `trigger.newmap` and `trigger.oldmap`. These are maps with the ID as the key in the record as the Valley. It's important to note that these trigger context variables are only available during certain contexts. For instance, you will not have a `trigger.old` variable during a before `insert` trigger. Additionally, you will not have access to newmap or oldmap containing `Id` until after `insert`. While this seems logically intuitive, it can often trip up developers who are used to accessing records by ID from amount or by ID for certain logic behaviors.

An example trigger

Let's start off our work with an example trigger that is relatively straightforward. We will be working on a trigger that updates a related record via its lookup. In this situation, we will be updating a case whenever the contact is updated. You can imagine this trigger being useful whenever we have a call-center-type situation and we want to update the case to reflect the contact's current phone number whenever the contact's information is updated. However, before we start writing the code for this trigger, let's think through the context of this trigger.

First, we should decide which DML statement will fire our trigger. For this example, we will be firing our trigger on a DML statement of update. Why update? Because we'll likely already have a contact record associated with this case. Whenever the contact record changes, we will update the case. We want to fire our trigger on contact because that's the object we want the trigger to reflexively act on. With those decisions behind us, we know two-thirds of our context. Then, the only question left is, do we want to do this before or after the record is saved? At the end of a `before` trigger, the records are automatically saved. On the other hand, `after` triggers do not automatically save the records. Because the `before` triggers finish by saving the record, it's best practice to write your triggers as `before` triggers whenever possible. However, when updating an object that is different than the one the trigger fired on, an `after` trigger may make more sense. For instance, our example trigger fires when a contact is updated, but makes changes to a case record. Because of this, we likely want an `after-update` context for our example trigger. This ensures that we'll have the latest information in our contact record when we start changing our case record. Keeping little details, such as when the data is automatically persisted, in mind can be the hardest part of writing triggers. However, evaluating the proper context, especially the timeframe aspect, is the the most crucial part to triggers.

For our example trigger, we want to update the case record whenever the contact record is updated. This allows us to ensure that the most current phone number is available to the case owner, for example. However, any changes to the case record have the potential of firing other triggers or chains of triggers that potentially update the contact object again. This is called a recursive, cyclical, or re-entrant trigger. Let's look at the following figure as an example:

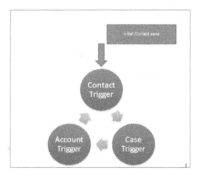

We can prevent most cyclical triggers using a static class variable as a semaphore. Simply create a simple class containing a `public static Boolean variable hasExecuted`, statement as follows:

```
Public static class triggerExecutionSemaphore {
Public static Boolean hasExecuted = false;
}
```

Then, in your trigger, check for the status of `hasExecuted` like this:

```
if (TriggerExecutionSemaphore.hasExecuted == false) {
  //continue with trigger logic
  triggerExecutionSemaphore = true;
}
```

As you might imagine, this method of preventing cyclical triggers can become cumbersome especially, as the number of triggers on the same object increases.

 This is something you wouldn't necessarily need to use a trigger for; however, it is a good example for the use of trigger. Later in this chapter, we will get more into more detail on when and why you should use a trigger.

Let's try the following code snippet as another example of a trigger:

```
Trigger UpdateContactPhoneNumberOnCase on Contact (after update) {
  List<Case> affectedCases = [SELECT id, mainContactPhone__c
          FROM Case
          WHERE contactId = :trigger.new[0].id];

  if(trigger.old[0].phone != trigger.new[0].phone) {
    for(Case thisCase: affectedCases) {
       thisCase.mainContactPhone__c = trigger.new[0].phone;
       update thisCase;
    }
  }
}
```

In this version of the trigger, we define our context on the first line. We name it `UpdateContactPhoneNumberOnCase` and specify that it should fire after contacts are updated. The first thing this trigger does, after defining the context, is make a SOQL query for cases whose contact ID matches contacts that were just updated. Finally, our trigger loops through the affected cases; if the new phone number is different than the old, we change the case with the new phone number and update it. In this trigger, we simply take the first record passed in from the `trigger context variable Trigger.new` context, update the related cases using our trigger logic, and then update the case record. Conceptually, this is exactly what a trigger is meant to do. It reflexively affects other records whenever our contact record changes. While this trigger functions, it has several issues, most notably that it only updates cases where the contact is the first record in the incoming `Trigger.new list` context.

Safety in numbers

Now we have a basic trigger under our belt. Let's look at what might happen if we fire that trigger with one record. If this trigger fires with a single contact record, it will update every case related to that contact whenever the contact's phone number is changed. However, triggers rarely run with only one record, and because of this, our example trigger has a number of flaws. If the trigger executes with two records, this trigger will only modify those cases where the contact ID matches the first contact record. However, the Salesforce1 platform *does not* guarantee that our triggers will fire with a single record. In fact, with this platform, it is quite clear that triggers will execute with at least 1 but no more than 200 records at a time. Because of this, we have to write our triggers to handle up to 200 records at a time. It may seem odd that 1 trigger would have to handle 200 records being updated at the same time, but remember that any code that inserts a list of records will fire a trigger with all of those records in it. For instance, the admin has just loaded 150 accounts via the data loader or a managed package updates a list of 199 contacts. Therefore, we have to write our triggers in such a way that we can handle 200 records at a time. However, 200 is our upper limit. If, for instance, a batch class has updated 400 records, the trigger would execute twice, once with the first 200, the second time with the second 200. This idea is called **bulk safety**. Writing triggers to be bulk safe involves ensuring that you handle your data and your trigger logic in a way that doesn't require extra database queries or DML statements. Let's take a look at the another example:

```
Trigger UpdateContactPhoneNumberOnCase on Contact (after update) {
    // Almost the same query as before,
// but we're going to process the list first
    // Note how we're using an In clause to get cases where
//the contactid is any of the contacts that were updated.
    List<Case> affectedCases = [SELECT id, mainContactPhone__c
          FROM Case
          WHERE contactId in
:trigger.newMap.keyset()];

    // This is the primary data structure we'll use to
// access our data.
    // A map of contact id's -> to list of cases.
    Map<id, List<Case>> affectedCasesByContactId = new Map<Id,
      List<Case>>();
    // Now to populate our map
    for(Case c: affectedCases) {
    if(affectedCasesByContactId.keyset().containsKey(c.contactId)){
      affectedCasesByContactId.get(c.contactId).add(c);
      } else {
```

```
      affectedCasesByContactId.put(c.contactId, new List<Case>{c});
    }
  }


  // create a new list to hold our newly updated cases
  // this way we can insert them all at once at the end.
  List<Case> updatedCases = new List<Case>();
  for(Id contactId: trigger.newMap.keyset()) {
  // Trap to make sure that the contact id we're working with
    actually
  // changed information we care about ie: the phone number.
    if(trigger.old.get(contactId).phone != trigger.new.get(contactId).
phone) {
      for(Case thisCase: affectedCasesByContactId.get(contactId)) {
      // Update all the cases to with the new phone number
      thisCase.mainContactPhone__c =
        trigger.new.get(contactId).phone;
      // add them to our list that we'll update.
      updatedCases.add(thisCase);
      }
    }
  }


  // Always wrap your DML in try/catch blocks.
  try {
    update updatedCases;
  } catch(Exception e) {
    System.debug(e.getMessage());
  }


}
```

This version of the trigger is much better. It is capable of handling multiple incoming contact records, and we've moved our DML to update the affected cases to the very end and updating them all at once as a list of records. Together, these modifications make our trigger bulk safe.

Note how we're using Map as a data structure for linking contact ids and their associated cases. There are three key takeaways here. First, we pull all the data needed from the database at the beginning of the trigger. Next, use lists of records for all DML calls. Lastly, keep all DML outside of loops. It's normal to loop over the individual items in a list to accomplish any logic or record manipulation but we need to ensure that our DML calls remain outside such loops. In fact, when writing triggers, keep all SOQL and DML outside all loops.

Infinite cosmic power, itty bitty safety rope

As I said before, triggers on the Force.com platform are incredibly flexible. That flexibility comes at the cost of safety and structure. Aside from the basic syntax of a trigger header `Trigger UpdateContactPhoneNumberOnCase on Contact (after update) {`, there are no hard and fast rules we have to follow. This often leads to objects having multiple, long, or complex triggers. Among the many freedoms you have with triggers, you have the ability to create multiple triggers on the same object. For instance, you can have 2 or 200 triggers on the account object. As your org grows through the years, you can imagine the number of triggers on the same object rising, not declining. However, imagine a scenario where over the course of 5 years, your company has built five triggers on the account object and you're tasked with fixing a bug—which of the triggers do you look at? Hopefully, the filenames are helpful, but realistically, you're now sifting through several files to reproduce, identify, and fix the bug.

Additionally, traditional trigger development on the Force.com platform places the logic for the trigger within the body of the trigger itself. Triggers, by their nature, often solve complex problems. If you combine multiple triggers on the same object along with classes called by those triggers, you're looking at potentially hundreds of thousands of lines of code. Or, as I like to call it—a maintenance nightmare. The fact that you don't know what order those triggers run in only complicates debugging and development. Preventing a cyclical or re-entrant trigger becomes much more difficult and important for data integrity.

Lastly, traditional trigger development creates a testability nightmare. Instead of unit testing the logic apart from mechanics of the reflex, we have to functionally test the trigger and its action. In other words, we have to set up some records and run a DML statement that fires the trigger just to check whether the logic we wrote successfully functioned as intended. With our reflex analogy, this makes sense. Actually, firing the trigger is like asking to be hit on the knee with a hammer. But we can safely assume that the reflex will fire—that's a platform feature. What we really care about is what happens after the hammer hits home—the logic of our trigger. Does the knee jerk *in the right direction*? Does the reflex affect *other objects as intended*? From this perspective, it would be better if we could test our trigger logic in isolation from the platform's trigger mechanism. Thankfully, there are a few simple rules that can help keep triggers well-structured and easy to maintain. They help ensure that we don't run into a nondeterministic order of firing situation and to unit test the logic. Our first rule, **Rule #1, Use a framework**.

The SFDC-trigger-framework

A couple of years ago, Salesforce MVP Kevin O'Hara released on GitHub the SFDC-trigger-framework. You can find it at `https://github.com/kevinohara80/sfdc-trigger-framework`. There are a number of trigger frameworks available for the platform, but this one is my favorite and the one I highly recommend. Since SFDC-trigger-framework is a bit of a mouthful, I will refer to it as the framework. The framework allows us to separate the logic from triggers in a way that allows us to create a deterministic order for those triggers to fire, and in a better way, for us to test the logic triggers. Because the trigger interface is controlled by Salesforce, very little of the actual trigger file will be different than traditional trigger development. Specifically, we still have to determine the context of our trigger and specify that in the trigger file for salesforce:

```
trigger AccountTrigger on Account (before insert, before update,
  before delete, after insert, after update, after delete, after
  undelete) {
  new AccountTriggerHandler().run();
}
```

You'll notice a few differences in this trigger definition, namely that it includes all possible timeframes and DML statements. You'll also see that it calls the `run` method of the `AccountTriggerHandler` class. This effectively causes the trigger to fire on all possible account contexts and call the `Run()` method. We do this so that our trigger logic, which exists in its own dedicated class, can determine whether or not it should run, when it should run, and in what order its components should run. This also introduces **Rule #2, Only one trigger per object**. Using a framework like this one allows us to have a single trigger per object because the logic is separated into its own class, which is **Rule #3: Triggers should contain no logic** — only exercising logic in another class. Ideally, we have triggers that run in all possible contexts and contain no logic!

The framework makes this crazy sounding idea possible by providing a series of methods that we can override. Our handler class will extend the framework provided by the `TriggerHandler` class. This provides the following methods that we can overwrite:

- `beforeInsert()`
- `beforeUpdate()`
- `beforeDelete()`
- `afterInsert()`
- `afterUpdate()`
- `afterDelete()`
- `afterUndelete()`

Our override methods allow us to determine what, if any, code is run before or after any given DML statement. When combined with an object, these seven methods cover all possible trigger contexts. The trigger framework handles determining the DML and timeframe, and it only calls methods that match context of this execution instance. While the trigger will always fire in every context, the framework ensures that only the code matching the current context runs. Thus, only the code referenced by the `beforeInsert()` method is called before the account is inserted, and only the code referenced by the `afterUpdate()` method is called after the update completes.

A cautionary note

While it may be tempting to put your logic directly inside these methods, it's better to think of these overriden methods (`beforeInsert()` and others) as dispatch methods, that is, methods that call other classes or methods. For instance, in the `beforeInsert()` method, you might call an `accountLib.sanitizeAccountData()` method followed by the `caseLib.createCase()` and `OpportunityLib.createOpp()` methods. Or you can call private helper methods found within the `AccountTriggerHandler` itself. This dispatch technique allows you *to deterministically order the logic your trigger executes within a given DML context*. For instance, your `beforeInsert()` override method might look something like this:

```
public class AccountTriggerHandler extends triggerHandler {
  public override void beforeInsert() {
    AccountLib.sanitizeDataForAccounts(Trigger.new);
    ContactLib.createContacts(Trigger.new);
    OpportunityLib.createOpps(Trigger.new);
  }
}
```

Rule #3 states that the triggers' logic should exist, not in the trigger, but in standard classes. Using this framework means buying into this idea wholeheartedly. Mixing in-trigger logic and class-based logic called by this framework negates the maintainability gains the framework provides. Regardless of whether or not you ever utilize this particular framework, placing your logic inside of a class and having the trigger call that class is an architectural and testing best practice. This makes the code more maintainable in the long run as you can edit classes and test classes more efficiently and deeply.

The framework is very lightweight, imposing few restrictions on developers. You can name your logic class anything you like but the convention created by Kevin O'Hara, and the one used in this book, is to call them trigger handlers. Therefore, if you have a trigger on the `Account` object, you would have an `accountTriggerHandler` class to dispatch the logic.

Using the framework

Because the methods in the `TriggerHandler` class are ultimately invoked during an Apex trigger context, they have access to the trigger context variables such as `Trigger.new` and `Trigger.old`. Additionally, if the context supports it, you'll have access to `Trigger.newMap` and `Trigger.oldMap`. While you have access to these collections in the `TriggerHandler` class, you must cast them to typed collections. This is required because Apex actually returns a collection of generic sObjects rather than collections of sObject subclasses, such as `Account`, `Opportunity` and so on. With this in mind, it's a good idea to use the constructor of your trigger handler to set a few class level variables that are precast to the object your handler works with, as follows:

```
public class AccountTriggerHandler extends triggerHandler {

  List<Account> triggerOld;
  Map<id, Account> triggerNewMap;
  Map<id, Account> triggerOldMap;

  public AccountTriggerHandler(){
    this.triggerNew = (List<Account>) trigger.new;
    this.triggerOld = (List<Account>) trigger.old;

    if(trigger.oldMap != null) {
      this.triggerOldMap = (Map<Id, Account>) trigger.oldMap;
    }
    if(trigger.newMap != null) {
      this.triggerNewMap = (Map<Id, Account>) trigger.NewMap;
    }
  }
}
```

Aside from encouraging you to clean up your logic and put it in the classes, the framework has a couple of other benefits that make writing triggers within the framework much easier and much more maintainable. Earlier, I talked about re-entrant or circular triggers, these are triggers fired by object 1 that does some sort of DML on object 2 which in turn does DML on object 1 causing the trigger on object 1 to reset and start the cycle all over again. For example, imagine a contact trigger that updates a case, which in turn updates an account, which in turn updates all the account's contacts. This of course would start the cycle over again. To prevent this, the framework has the ability to keep track of how many times the trigger has been fired. Once the threshold for execution has been exceeded, the framework will throw an exception. This is called the **max loop count** API. To use it, call the `setMaxLoopCount(X)` method. This method is provided by the framework and accepts one integer argument. When the trigger execution count hits that number, it will throw an exception:

```
public class ContactTriggerHandler extends TriggerHandler {
  public ContactTriggerHandler() {
    this.setMaxLoopCount(2);
  }
}
```

Perhaps most importantly, the framework provides a way for developers to selectively, and programmatically disable triggers. The one caveat to this is that the bypassed triggers must also use the framework. Essentially, this allows developers to prevent re-entrant or cyclical triggers by disabling triggers on demand. In other words, if you fire a trigger on an account and you know that that will also result in a contact trigger running, you can bypass the execution of the contact trigger programmatically from your account trigger. This is accomplished with a set of two methods:

```
TriggerHandler.bypass('AccountTriggerHandler');
TriggerHandler.clearBypass('AccountTriggerHandler');
```

Whenever you'd like to bypass a trigger's execution, call the `TriggerHandler.bypass` method with the name of the *trigger handler* you'd like to bypass. When you've completed your potentially re-entrant DML, call the `TriggerHandler.clearBypass()` method with the name of the trigger handler you previously bypassed. This feature is incredibly powerful and when combined with the `maxLoopCount` API, provides a robust way to prevent re-entrant triggers.

Let's take a look at what our example trigger would look like if we wrote it with the trigger framework.

First, this is what the actual trigger source would look like:

```
trigger AccountTrigger on Account (before insert, before update,
before delete, after insert, after update, after delete, after
undelete) {
  new AccountTriggerHandler().run();
}
```

The `AccountTriggerHandler` class would look like this:

```
public class AccountTriggerHandler extends triggerHandler {

  List<Account> triggerNew;
  List<Account> triggerOld;
  Map<id, Account> triggerNewMap;
  Map<id, Account> triggerOldMap;

  Public AccountTriggerHandler(){
    this.triggerNew = (List<Account>) trigger.new;
```

```
    this.triggerOld = (List<Account>) trigger.old;

    if(trigger.oldMap != null) {
      this.triggerOldMap = (Map<Id, Account>) trigger.oldMap;
    }
    if(trigger.newMap != null) {
      this.triggerNewMap = (Map<Id, Account>) trigger.newMap;
    }
}

@testVisible
Private AccountTriggerHandler(list<Account>
  newMockAccountsForTesting, list<Account>
  oldMockAccountsForTesting){
    this.triggerNew = newMockAccountsForTesting;
    this.triggerOld = oldMockAccountsForTesting;
}

public override void afterUpdate() {
    doUpdate(updateCasesWithNewContactPhoneIfChanged());
}

private void doUpdate(List<Account> toInsert){
    // Always wrap your DML in try/catch blocks.
    try {
      update toInsert;
    } catch(Exception e) {
      System.debug(e.getMessage());
    }
}

@testVisible
private List<Case> updateCasesWithNewContactPhoneIfChanged(){
 List<Case> affectedCases = [SELECT id, mainContactPhone__c
        FROM Case
        WHERE contactId in :triggerNewMap.keyset()];

// This is the primary data structure we'll use to access our data.
  // A map of contact id's -> to list of cases.
  Map<id, List<Case>> affectedCasesByContactId = new Map<Id,
    List<Case>>();
  // Now to populate our map
  for(Case c: affectedCases) {
```

```
            if(affectedCasesByContactId.keyset().containsKey(c.contactId)){
            affectedCasesByContactId.get(c.contactId).add(c);
            } else {
            affectedCasesByContactId.put(c.contactId, new List<Case>{c});
                }
        }


        // create a new list to hold our newly updated cases
        // this way we can insert them all at once at the end.
        List<Case> updatedCases = new List<Case>();
        for(Id contactId: trigger.newMap.keyset()) {
            // Trap to make sure that the contact id we're working with
              actually
            // changed information we care about ie: the phone number.
          if(trigger.old.get(contactId).phone !=
            trigger.new.get(contactId).phone) {
          for(Case thisCase: affectedCasesByContactId.get(contactId)) {
            // Update all the cases to with the new phone number
            thisCase.mainContactPhone__c =
                trigger.new.get(contactId).phone;
          // add them to our list that we'll update.
              updatedCases.add(thisCase);
            }
          }
        }


        return updatedCases;


    }
}
```

Finally, our trigger tests can now test the logic of the
updateCasesWithNewContactPhoneIfChanged() method without necessitating
waiting for DML statements to finish. Our Test class looks like this:

```
@isTest
private class ProfitStarsUtils_Tests {

  @isTest static void test_updateCasesWithNewContactPhoneIfChanged() {
    List<Account> accountsToTestWith = TestUtils.
generateListOfAccounts(5);
    List<Account> newAccountsToTestWith = new List<Account>();
    for (Account a: accountsToTestWith) {
     a.phone = '555 867 5300';
    }
```

```
// this invokes the private constructor that's only visible
  to tests
AccountTriggerHandler a = new
  AccountTriggerHandler(newAccountsToTestWith,
  accountsToTestWith);
Test.startTest();
List<Account> results =
  a.updateCasesWithNewContactPhoneIfChanged();
Test.stopTest();
system.assertEquals(results.size(), 5, 'expected to have 5
  accounts in collection');
for (Account a : results) {
  system.assertEquals(a.mainContactPhone__c, '555 867 5309',
    'expected the new phone number to be set as the
    mainContactPhone__c');
  }
 }

}
```

Summary

In this chapter, we rehashed the basics of trigger development on the Force.com platform. Additionally, we talked about trigger frameworks and investigated one of them — the SFDC-trigger-framework by Kevin O'Hara — in depth. Hopefully, you're comfortable reading and writing basic triggers, know the risks inherent in traditional trigger development and how a framework like Kevin O'Hara's helps impart order and discipline to triggers.

In the next chapter, we'll take a look at using various forms of asynchronous Apex, such as batchable and schedulable Apex as well as `@future` annotated code and the new queueable Apex classes.

3
Asynchronous Apex for Fun and Profit

In this chapter, we will focus on processing large amounts of data. We'll talk about the batchable interface as well as its options and how we can schedule batch jobs using a corresponding schedulable interface. We will talk about the `@future` annotation for methods and the new Queueable interface. All told we will cover:

- Batchable
- Schedulable
- Queueable
- The `@future` annotation

Using batchable classes

Collectively referred to as **asynchronous code** batchable, queueable, and the `@future` methods contract a tradeoff with the Salesforce1 platform. In exchange for running the code asynchronously, meaning we have no control over when it's actually executed, the platform relaxes certain governor limitations. For instance, during normal, synchronous Apex execution, you are limited to modifying 10,000 records per DML call. Attempting to access more than 10,000 records throws a SOQL error. However, during the execution of a batchable class, those governor limits are reset every time the execute method is called.

Conceptually, asynchronous code executes in two steps. First, the code is queued. As system resources allow, the system pulls jobs off the queue and executes them. As usual, the devil is in the details. Batchable, Queueable, and the `@future` annotation all have various tradeoffs that distinguish them from each other. Knowing when to use which one is crucial. As we work through each of the options, we'll talk about appropriate use cases for each.

For batchable jobs, there is an intermediary step between queuing and execution: chunking. When you execute your batch job, the system runs the initial query and chunks up the results, enqueueing N number of jobs—one job for every X number of results. The X factor is the batch execution context, or the number of records that each batch will process. As the developer, you can specify what the branch execution context is when you start the job. If left unspecified, it defaults to 200 records per chunk.

The `Database.batchable` interface, provided by the platform is straightforward. Simply extended your class with `Database.Batchable`, like this:

```
public with sharing class myBatchable extends Database.batchable
```

Once you've extended `Database.batchable`, you're required to implement the three method signatures the interface requires. The first of the three required methods is the `Start` method, which the platform calls at the beginning of batch's overall execution:

```
global Database.QueryLocator start(Database.BatchableContext BC) {
  return Database.getQueryLocator([
SELECT IDId, FirstName, LastName, BillingAddress
    FROM Account
    WHERE Active = true AND BillingState = 'Tx'
    ORDER BY Id descDESC
  ]);
}
```

This first method gathers the records or objects that the `execute` method will act on and, in conjunction with the execution context, determines the number of chunks that will be executed. The `start` method provides two possible return values, either a `Database.queryLocator` object or an iterable object, such as a `List`. The preceding example uses `queryLocator`. Regardless of the type returned, it must accept a single parameter of the `Database.BatchableContext` type. When the `execute` method is called, it returns an ID, which you can use to query the `AsyncApexJob` object. The `AsyncApexJob` object gives you insight into the status of a batch job:

```
global void execute(Database.BatchableContext BC, List<Account> scope)
{
  for (Account a : scope) {
    //Complex operations against individual
//Account records here
  }
  update scope;
}
```

The `Database.batchableContext BC` variable is essentially dependency injected by the system. However, our second method, the `execute` method, must reference it to fulfill the batchable interface. The `execute` method is run once per chunk. It accepts not only `Database.batchableContext`, but also a chunk of records; a list of whatever object the `start()` method returns. In the preceding example code, I've called that chunk `scope`, and in this case, it's a list of the `Account` objects. Because the `execute` method is called once per chunk, scope is essentially a local iteration variable. Thankfully, the platform dependency injects a chunk into every execute call; meaning we're not responsible for running the `execute()` calls ourselves.

The general pattern for a batchable class `execute` method is to iterate over the given scope using a `for`. In general, this for loop is where you implement your custom business logic either by placing the logic there in the execute method, or better yet, calling a dedicated class method much like we talked about with triggers. While you modify individual records inside the `for` loop, like a trigger, you must keep DML outside of your loop! Loop over your scope records, modify them, and then insert/update/delete, and so on, all of them at once just after the loop ends. If you need to use the loop to determine what kind of DML ultimately happens to the records, do so with multiple lists. For instance, if you're iterating over a scope of accounts and determining which of them to delete, create an additional list and use that to delete those records in bulk as shown here:

```
global void execute(Database.BatchableContext BC, List<Account> scope)
{
  List<Account> toDelete = new List<Account>();
  List<Account> toUpdate = new List<Account>();

  for (Account a : scope) {
    if(a.bad_account__c){
      toDelete.add(a);
    } else {
      toUpdate.add(a);
    }
  }
  update toUpdate;
  delete toDelete;
}
```

In this example, we're not actually updating the scope directly, but rather splitting the records into two lists. One to delete, one to update, and only then calling the appropriate DML after the loop is finished.

Of all the methods of the `batchableBatchable` class, the `execute` method is conceptually the most straightforward. However, it's often the most difficult to perfect. It pays to keep in mind the governor limits affecting batchable class execution. While asynchronous Apex, such as jobs conforming to the batchable interface, relax some governor limits, your `execute` method is still limited to 10k rows per DML call. If, for instance, you utilize the increased memory you have available to access to more than 10k, you'll hit governor limits even if you use the bulk pattern discussed earlier. On the other hand, if you're executing SOQL queries within your execute method, but outside your for loop, you're bound by the standard governor limits, they just reset every time the `execute` method is invoked.

The third method in the batchable interface is the `finish()` method. The `finish` method is run after the `start()` method has queued all of the chunks and those chunks have been executed. The general idea is that after your batch job is functionally completed, the `finish` method can send e-mail notifications to users or handle execution exceptions. In general, such cleanup tasks should rarely rely on specific data, but can reliably rely on the jobs execution to be complete. For instance, if you use a batch job to look at all of your opportunity records in order to sum the value of all records meeting a certain criteria, your `finish()` method would be responsible for persisting the summary record.

Knowing what to use the `finish` method for can be one the most confusing aspects of the `batchableBatchable` Apex classes. It is safe to use the `finish()` method for things that are guaranteed to have run. However, it is not safe to depend upon any data generated by the batch. This is because the data generated by an execute method may not always exist. Exceptions within the `execute()` method force a roll back of any DML thus, if an exception occurs, the data you expect may not actually be there when your finish method runs. On the other hand, knowing when to use a batch class is fairly straightforward. Use batch class when you need to carry out the same logic against a large number of records; specifically, more than 10,000 records. Using a `Database.Batchable` class allows you to access or modify up to 50 million records per `queryLocator`. At a maximum DML chunk size of 10,000, this means your batchable class will queue 5000 chunks.

Additional extensions

Batchable classes can implement two additional interfaces: `Database.Stateful` and `Database.AllowsCallouts`. Implementing these two interfaces is as simple as adding them to your `batchableBatchable` class signature, as follows:

```
Global Class CustomBatchable Implements
Database.Batchable<sObject>,
Database.Stateful, // This implements the Stateful interface
Database.AllowsCallouts { // This enables Callouts
}
```

The `Database.Stateful` interface allows you to maintain state across all of the execute method invocations. The crucial difference is that when `Database.stateful` is implemented, instance variables *are not* reset each time the execute method is called. This is incredibly useful, for example, if you want to maintain a summary of calculations. Previously, I talked about the hypothetical example where we iterated over all our opportunities to calculate a sum if those opportunities met certain criteria. The `Database.Stateful` interface makes this simple. Simply add `Database.stateful` to the list of interfaces and create an instance variable like this:

```
global double totalSum =0;
```

During your execution method, simply add to the `totalSum` variable, and then in your `finish` method, write that sum to the database. Because class instance variables are not reset when `Database.stateful` is implemented, we can simply add to the instance variable in the execution method. That instance variable is also available in the finish method for persisting to the database. Another classic use case for implementing `Database.Stateful` is error handling. Exceptions within the `execute` method result in a rollback of that invocations scope. If you wish to allow partial scope updating while also capturing records that fail, you must implement `Database.Stateful` and use `Database.update()` for DML updates. There are two key parts to this recipe.

First, DML updates must be done with the `Database.update()` method with the optional `AllOrNone` flag set to `false`. This will allow some records to fail, while updating others. The `Database.update()` method returns a `Database.saveResult` object—a list indicating which records succeeded or failed.

Secondly, in order to maintain a list of failed records for processing later, you need to implement `Database.Stateful` and create an instance list variable to hold your failed records. Once all of the execute invocations have completed, your `finish()` method can access or manipulate the list of failed records. This is an incredibly useful pattern as it allows you a clean path for updating records in bulk while handling exceptions!

Here is an example of a `customBatchable` class that implements `Database.Stateful` to capture specific record. Ensure that you read the comments dispersed throughout that explain what's happening:

```
Global Class CustomBatchable implements
    Database.Batchable<sObject>, Database.Stateful,
    Database.AllowsCallouts {
    //failedToUpdate persists throughout the entire job.
    Private Set<Account> failedToUpdate = new Set<Account>();
    //Because it's marked Static, updatedSuccessfully
    // resets every time the execute method runs
```

```
Private Static Set<Id> updatedSuccessfully = new Set<Id>();
String query;

global CustomBatchable() {
  //Optional constructor, useful for setting query
  //variables like Dates etc. Setting the query in the
  // constructor allows you to use dynamic SOQL as well
  this.query = 'SELECT IDId, Name, BillingStreet, BillingState
  FROM Account ORDER BY Id DESC';
}

global Database.QueryLocator start(Database.BatchableContext BC) {
  return Database.getQueryLocator(query);
}

global void execute(Database.BatchableContext BC, List<Account>
  scope) {
  for (Account a : scope) {
    if (a.BillingState == 'Tx' || a.Name.contains('awesome')) {
      a.Active__c = 'true';
    }
  }
  Database.SaveResult[] results = Database.Update(scope, false);

  for (Database.SaveResult sr : results) {
    if (sr.isSuccess()) {
      updatedSuccessfully.add(sr.getId());
    }
  }

  for (Account a : scope) {
    if (!updatedSuccessfully.contains(a.Id)) {
      failedToUpdate.add(a);
    }
  }
}

global void finish(Database.BatchableContext BC) {
  if (failedToUpdate.size() > 0) {
    //Email admin about failed updates
    //Or process them individually, attempting to
    //auto-correct DML issues.
  }
  //Once done processing the failed records:
```

```
        List<Account> insertNow = new List<Account>();
        insertNow.addAll(failedToUpdate);
        insert insertNow;
    }
}
```

Note how the `execute` method references both a class instance variable, `failedToUpdate`, and a class static variable, `updatedSuccessfully`. The static variable, `updatedSuccessfully`, resets every time the `execute` method is run, but the instance variable, `failedToUpdate` does not. This allows us to add records to the instance variable whenever an object fails to update. In the case of our preceding example class, we use `updatedSuccessfully` to build a temporary set of IDs the `SaveResult` object lists as successfully updated. Then, we compare the `set` of successfully updated records against the full list of records we attempted to update. Those records whose `id` is not in the `successfullyUpdated` set are added to the `FailedToUpdate` set that persists across all execution runs. When all the batches are executed, the `finish` method acts on those records in the `FailedToUpdate` set.

If your batch job needs to make callouts to external web services you'll need to write your batch class to implement `Database.AllowsCallouts`. Thankfully, like the `Database.Stateful` interface, you only need to add `Database.AllowsCallouts` to your class definition. Also, note that your callout logic does not need to directly reside inside your batch class. Indeed, you should implement your callouts in their own classes and call that code from within your batchable class. That said, if your batch class invokes code that makes a callout, you must implement `Database.AllowsCallouts`.

There are a few governor caveats to implement `Database.AllowsCallouts`. While your `execute` method resets governor limits, you are still limited to a maximum of 100 callouts per invocation. If you are working with a batch execution context of 200 or 2000, this means that your callouts have to be bulk safe, as making a callout for each of the 200 records would necessarily cause a governor limit exception. Alternatively, if the web service you are calling is not bulk safe and requires a 1:1 call per record, you must set your execution context size to `100` or lower. However, this will limit the number of records you can process overall, so ensure that you embed some sort of `processed` flag in your data model and initial query so that you can execute the batch job multiple times. Again, remember that while you can make callouts in the `start()` and `finish()` methods, each method is limited to a total of 100 callouts.

Regardless of whether your batchable class implements `Database.Sateful` or `Database.allowsCallouts`, all batchable classes are executed by running the `Database.executeBatch()` method and providing both an instance of the batchable class and the query execution context as an integer as shown here:

```
Id batchJobId = Database.executeBatch(new CustomBatchable(), 200);
```

The resulting Id object helps you find the status of the batch. Batch jobs can also be scheduled using the System.schedule() method, but it should be noted that System.schedule() runs as the system user, executing all classes whether or not the user has permission. Alternatively, you can use a schedulable class to start your batch job via Database.executeBatch().

Schedulable classes

As a companion to batchable interface, the Salesforce platform provides a schedulable interface. Schedulable classes are considered as asynchronous Apex, because the platform merely adds the job to the queue at the scheduled time. It does not promise that the job will actually run at the scheduled time, but it does promises that it will be queued at that time. The actual processing may take place nearly instantaneously, or at some point in the relatively near future, depending on system resource availability. Using the schedulable interface allows you to queue code at specific times or periodic intervals. This can be implemented either through the web user interface, or through apex code. Like the batchable interface, to utilize the schedulable functionality, you must implement the schedulable interface by implementing the execute() method. The execute() method must accept a single variable of the SchedulableContext type. Like it's Batchable cousin, SchedulableContext is dependency injected by the system. Here is the definition of a simple schedulable class that invokes a batch job:

```
global class SchedulableClass implements Schedulable {
  global void execute(SchedulableContext SC) {
    // do stuff here.
  }
}
```

One of the benefits of the schedulable class interface is that you can use it to trigger batch jobs. Schedulable classes in conjunction with batch jobs enable you to run code at a specific time, while still iterating over massive amounts of data and making callouts as necessary. However, executing batch jobs is not its only feature. By itself, the scheduler can trigger specific code from any class, including itself, to run. However, using the schedulable class to invoke a batch job frees you from certain governor limits. Specifically, schedulable classes do not allow you to make callouts and are limited by standard DML and SOQL limits. However, when you use a schedulable class to queue a batch job, that batch job can make callouts, if it implements Database.AllowsCallouts. Likewise, calling a batch job, also let's you manipulate massive data sets. For instance, if you need to run the opportunity batch job, which we spoke of earlier, on a daily basis, you can use a schedulable class to call the opportunity batch job every day at 2am

Monitoring

The Salesforce platform provides a monitoring system for the Schedulable system. Within your execute method, you can call the `getTriggerId()` method on the `SchedulableContext` object passed into it. That method returns an `IDId` that you can use in conjunction with SOQL to query the `CronTrigger` object. Using SOQL and the `getTriggerId()` method, you can get the number of times this schedulable method has fired and the next time it is scheduled to fire. Additionally, you can navigate in the setup menu to **monitor | jobs | scheduled jobs** to view all the scheduled jobs!

Scheduling from Apex

To set the schedule of a class that implements schedulable from Apex, you use the `System.schedule()` method. The `System.Schedule()` method takes three arguments: a String containing the name of the job, a cron expression, and an instance of the schedulable class. Cron expressions are easily the hardest part of this scheduling. Cron expressions take the form of a string representing the time and date that the class should execute at in a seconds, minutes, hours format as well as the day of the month, month, day of the week and, optionally, the year. To complicate matters, cron expressions can include intervals, sets, keywords, and wildcards. The following are a few example cron expressions along with a plain English translation of what they represent.

This expression fires every hour on the hour, for all days, months, and years: 0 seconds, 0 minutes, of every hour, every day of the month, every month, no-set day of the week, with no optional year:

```
String EXAMPLE_CRON_EXPRESSION = '0 0 * * * ?';
```

Every hour, 10 minutes after the hour on all days in 2016: or 0 seconds into the 10th minute of every hour every day of the month, with no specific day of the week set, during 2015:

```
String EXAMPLE_CRON_EXPRESSION = '0 10 * * * ? 2016';
```

Runs Monday—Friday at 10am or: 0 seconds and 0 minutes into the 10 o'clock hour for unspecified days of the month, during all months for the range of days that are Monday-Friday:

```
String EXAMPLE_CRON_EXPRESSION = '0 0 10 ? * MON-FRI';
```

Runs on the last Friday of the month at 10pm, or 0 seconds, and 0 minutes of the 22nd hour on unspecified days of the week, for all months on the L (last) 6th day, that is: Friday:

```
String EXAMPLE_CRON_EXPRESSION = '0 0 22 ? * 6L';
```

Runs on the last weekday of each quarter at 10:40pm or: 0 seconds after the 40th minute of the 22nd hour on unspecified days of the month every 4 months starting with month 12 (December):

```
String EXAMPLE_CRON_EXPRESSION = '0 40 22 ? 12/4 6LW';
```

As you can tell, cron expressions can range from as simple as running code every hour on the hour to complex expressions that run on the last day of a given fiscal quarter. Once you have created your cron expression, you can schedule the job using the developer console's execute anonymous window, as follows:

```
Enter Apex Code                                                    ▲ ✕
1   String EXAMPLE_CRON_EXPRESSION = '0 10 * * * ? 2015';
2   System.schedule('The Dr\'s Scheduled Job',
3                   EXAMPLE_CRON_EXPRESSION,
4                   new CustomSchedulableClass());
5



                                    ☐ Open Log   Execute   Execute Highlighted
```

Note that the first argument to **System.schedule** is what will be displayed as the **Job Name** field on the **Scheduled Job** page. This page, found under **Setup | Monitor | Jobs | Scheduled Jobs**, allows you to cancel jobs that are scheduled as well as see how often jobs have run, and when each job will next run.

Testing schedulable classes

Testing schedulable classes generally follows this pattern. Create a cron expression specifically for testing with a fixed year far in the future, schedule the class with that cron expression, and finally make assertions against the number of times the job has run and the next scheduled time. Effectively this looks as follows:

```
@isTest
private class CustomScheduledClass_Test {
```

```
@isTest static void test_withCronExpressionForOneYearInFuture() {
   Integer oneYearInFuture = Date.today().addYears(1).year();
   String TESTING_CRON_EXPRESSION = '0 0 0 15 3 ? ' +
      oneYearInFuture;

   Test.startTest();
   String JobIdentifier = System.Schedule('The Best Job Ever',
      TESTING_CRON_EXPRESSION, new CustomBatchableClass());

   CronTrigger CronTriggerObj = [SELECT Id, CronExpression,
      TimesTriggered, NextFireTime
                              FROM CronTrigger
                              WHERE id = :JobIdentifier];

   System.assertEquals(CRON_EXP, CronTriggerObj.CronExpression);
   System.assertEquals(0, CronTriggerObj.TimesTriggered);
   System.assertEquals('2022-03-15 00:00:00',
      String.valueOf(CronTriggerObj.NextFireTime));
   Test.startTest();
   }
}
```

This pattern is predicated on a simple premise—that your schedulable class merely executes code from another class that is independently tested. This is the recommended path, if for no other reason than it separates the concerns of scheduling from business logic and facilitates rapid, efficient testing.

Exploring @future annotated methods

The `@future` annotation (pronounced as at future) is, perhaps, the simplest method of asynchronous code execution on the Salesforce1 platform. The `@future`, is a method annotation that makes the method run asynchronously at some point in the near future. Generally, this happens quite quickly, but no time guarantees are established annotation methods as `@future` is fantastically useful, but has a number of caveats and limitations that developers must remain mindful of:

- Most importantly, methods annotated with `@future` can only accept primitive parameter types. String, Integer, and so on, are your only options.

- You cannot chain methods annotated with `@future`. In other words, an `@future` annotated method cannot be called from another `@future` annotated method. This is especially crucial to remember when your `@future` method may result in a trigger firing. If an `@future` method fires a trigger, that trigger cannot in turn call other `@future` annotated methods.

- Methods annotated with @future *cannot* return a value — they must have a Void return type — and they must be declared static.

These caveats and limitations should not deter you from using the @future annotation. Indeed, the biggest limitation that — parameters must be primitives — can be easily overcome with a bit of clever programming. For example, while an @future method cannot take sObjects for parameters, it can accept a string. Even a string resulting from the JSON serialization of an sObject, or list of sObjects. The following is an example of this pattern:

```
Public with sharing class Examples {
  @future
  Public public Static Void void myAtFutureMethod(String
    jsonStringOfAccount){
    Account a = (Account) JSON.deserialize(jsonStringOfAccount,
      Account.class);
    //do work with your sObject
  }
}
```

One of the best features of the @future annotated methods is that they can be used to execute callouts. If, for instance, you are integrating with an external API that takes a while to return, you can make the callout from an @future method rather than, say, your Visualforce controller. To enable the callout feature of the @future methods, append the option callout=true to your @future annotation. Methods annotated with the @future annotations with callouts work best when you are creating net-new related records. If you are editing an existing record, you will likely end up in a situation where the @future method executes the DML to update the record. If there are triggers calling the @future methods set on the same object — a common enough occurrence — you will inadvertently end up throwing an exception trying to execute an @future method from within an @future context.

When to use the @future annotation on methods

In general, use the @future annotations on methods where the situation is truly fire-and-forget. Running code in a future context resets the governor limits by creating a new Apex context to run them in. If your code is encapsulated, such that you can execute a single method in a different Apex context, then it is fine to annotate it as @future. Be careful calling methods with the @future annotation from triggers.

Queueable classes

With the recent Spring '15 release, Apex developers have a new asynchronous tool, queueable Apex classes. At first glance, queueable classes are very similar to `@future` annotated methods. A closer look, however, reveals their true power. There are three key differences between `@future` and queueable classes:

- The method for enqueueing a job returns an ID, allowing you to monitor its progress much like a batch or scheduled job
- Queueable jobs accept `sObjects`
- Finally, and perhaps most importantly, queueable code can invoke queueable code — no more exceptions complaining about how you are trying to call the `@future` methods or batch methods from an `@future` context

Implementing the queueable interface is very similar to implementing the batchable or schedulable interfaces. Simply define your class as implementing the queueable interface and implement the `execute()` method. Likewise, your implementation of the `execute()` method must accept one argument of the `QueueableContext` type. This method does not have to be the only method in the class; in fact, you can use constructors and other methods as you see fit. The general pattern is to write the constructor so that it accepts `sObjects` and assigns them to class level instance variables. The `execute()` method is then used to implement asynchronous logic. Importantly, inside the `execute()` method, you can access the `JobId` by invoking the `getJobId()` method on the `QueueableContext` object that the system injects at runtime. With this `Id`, you can write SOQL queries to gather data about the object.

Perhaps the clearest real-world example of using the Queueable interface is doing a call out to a web service where you need to log both successes and failures. While an `@future` method is capable of making callouts, the Queueable interface is capable not only of callouts but also monitoring and, as of the Spring '15 release, automatically retrying. To help us log successes and failures, we will create a new `sObject` called `AuditLog__c`, with the following fields:

Field Type	Name	Purpose
Boolean	`Success__c`	Flag for success or failure
Long Text	`RequestJson__c`	JSON representation of the request
Long Text	`ResponseJson__c`	JSON representation of the server response
Id	`JobId__c`	ID of the async job
Long Text	`stacktrace__c`	Text of the Stacktrace
Id	`AccountId__c`	ID of the Account this audit log is relates too

Queueable jobs can be enqueued by calling System.enqueueJob() with an instance of our queueable class. In this case, we will instantiate our AuditLogGenerator queueable class with an Account object. Executing the System.enequeJob() method with an instance of our AuditLogGenerator class will return a jobId. Once the system picks up the job and calls the execute() method, we can query for the Audit Log record information with that jobId field. With both the account object passed in via the constructor and the auditlog__AuditLog__c record, we can make our callout while logging successes and failures as well as automated retries. Here is what that AuditLogGenerator class looks like:

```
Public with sharing class auditLogGenerator AuditLogGenerator
implements Queueable, Database.allowsCallouts {
  private account a {get; set;}
  public AuditLogGenerator(Account incomingAccount) {
    this.a = incomingAccount;
  }

  public void execute(QueueableContext qc) {
    Audit_Log__c log = [SELECT Id, Success__c, RequestJson__c,
ResponseJson__c, Stacktrace__c, AccountID__c
                    FROM Audit_Log__c
                    WHERE JobId__c = :qc.getJobId()];

    try {
      log.RequestJson__c =
        Rest.GenerateRequestFromAccount(this.a);
      HTTPResponse response =
Rest.makeRestRequestWithUrlMethodAndBody('https://www.example.com'
        , Rest.GET, log.RequestJson__c);

      if (response.getStatusCode() == 200) {
        log.Success__c = true;
      }
      log.ResponseJson__c = response.getBody();
    } catch (Exception e) {
      log.Success__c = false;
      log.Stacktrace__c = e.getStackTraceString();
    }
    if (!log.Success__c) {
      Id retryJobId = System.EnqueueJob(new
        auditLogGenerator(this.a));
      Audit_Log__c retryAuditLog = new Audit_Log__c(JobId__c =
        retryJobId, AccountID__c = this.a.Id);
    }
    update log;
  }
}
```

Testing Queueable classes

Testing Queueable classes is much like testing the `@future` methods. The only requirement is proper use of `Test.startTest()` and `Test.stopTest()`. The asynchronous code executed between `Test.startTest()` and `Test.stopTest()` methods is forced to run immediately when `Test.stopTest()` is called. This greatly simplifies testing. We need only to call our `System.EnqueueJob()` method between `Test.startTest()` and `Test.stopTest()` and make assertions as if it were synchronous, rather than asynchronous code. Consider the following example:

```
@isTest
private class AuditLogGenerator_Tests {

  static testmethod void test1() {
    Account firstAccount = (Account) TestFactory.createSObject(new
      Account());
    insert firstAccount;
    Audit_Log__c log;
    HTTPMockCalloutFactory fakeResponse = new
      HTTPMockCalloutFactory(200,
        'OK',
        '{"results":"Ok"}',
        new Map<String, String>()
    );
    Test.setMock(HttpCalloutMock.class, fakeResponse);

    Id jobId;
    Test.startTest();
      jobId = System.EnqueueJob(new
        auditLogGenerator(firstAccount));
      log = new Audit_Log__c(JobId__c = jobId, AccountID__c =
        firstAccount.Id);
    Test.stopTest();

    Audit_Log__c resultingLog = [SELECT success__c
                                 FROM Audit_Log__c
                                 WHERE jobId = :jobId];
    System.assert(resultingLog.success__c);
  }
}
```

As you can see in the preceding example, `Test.startTest()` and `Test.stopTest()` bracket our actual enqueueing code. This is all that's required to force the testing framework to run our asynchronous code synchronously within the execution flow of our test.

Knowing when to use what

Asynchronous Apex, in its various forms, is incredibly useful. By trading synchronous execution of your code for relaxed or reset governor limits, you can process massive numbers of records, call out to web services without holding up your users, and, as of the Spring '15 release, you can even write fault tolerant asynchronous callouts. Knowing when to use which type of Asynchronous Apex, however, can be difficult. With that in mind, here are some guidelines:

- If you are manipulating more than 2000 records, use Batchable Apex.

- While you can directly schedule Batchable Apex, it is almost always preferable to wrap the batch Apex execution in a scheduled class, as this provides much more flexibility regarding execution time and.

- Use the `@future` annotation in situations where the method can be called and forgotten.

- Default to Queueable Apex for asynchronous code, manipulating less than 2000 records at a time.

- Write and use a standard wrapper for Queueable Apex like the one we discussed previously to create fault-tolerant queues.

These guidelines are just guidelines, and each individual situation should be evaluated to determine the appropriate Asynchronous Apex pattern. Remember that each of these Asynchronous tools has their own set of tradeoffs and benefits. They all run when the system has resources available, but the `@future` methods, for instance, can only accept primitive data types and cannot be chained. On the other hand, batchable classes can be chained, and can handle larger sets of data. Schedulable Apex provides the most flexible way to repeatedly run asynchronous Apex with an incredibly flexible cron scheduler. Finally, Queueable Apex, while new, is easily the most flexible, especially with a wrapper class controlling it. Queueable Apex additionally provides the only fault-tolerant asynchronous solution for situations like callouts where the work must be completed, even if it takes a few tries!

Asynchronous Apex is easily one of the most powerful tools Force.com developers have at their disposal. Developers have to master the various asynchronous Apex techniques to unlock the true power of the platform. With asynchronous Apex machine learning, data mining and deep custom integrations with other systems are possible. Hopefully, this chapter has laid out a good understanding of the various patterns, but the real mastery of these patterns will come through practice and experience.

Summary

Throughout this chapter, we covered a great deal of technical information on the why and how of asynchronous development on the Salesforce1 platform. Additionally, we discussed the importance of knowing when to use which technique. These techniques will come in useful as you start dealing with API integrations and processing large numbers of records. But before we get to those topics, we need to stop and discuss Unit testing.

4
Lightning Concepts

If you've not come across it yet, you're sure to soon hear all about Salesforce Lightning. Lightning is an umbrella term covering at least four distinct technologies. This has led to a bit of confusion about what Lightning is. These technologies can be used in conjunction with one another, and they all share one thing in common—they help you build applications at Lightening speed. In this chapter, we'll talk about each of the following four technologies independently so that you'll be able to adopt them in your organization and deliver apps quickly:

- Lightning Process Builder
- Lightning Connect
- Lightning Components
- Lightning App Builder

The Lightning Process Builder

Workflow rules and actions are the bread and butter of Salesforce1 platform developers. When developing applications, declarative tools such as workflow rules allow fairly complex logic to be executed without writing code. There are, however, a number of limitations with workflow rules. The most frustrating limitation is that you cannot see an entire process of workflow rules on a single screen. Process Builder is easily the most powerful upgrade of the platform technology since s-controls were deprecated. While it's easy to consider Process Builder as a replacement for workflow rules (and it may get there), right now it can replace some but not all of your workflow rules. Process Builder encourages you to consider the entire process your data works through. Process Builder uses a UI that shows a series of criteria diamonds and action squares. A simple process might look something like this:

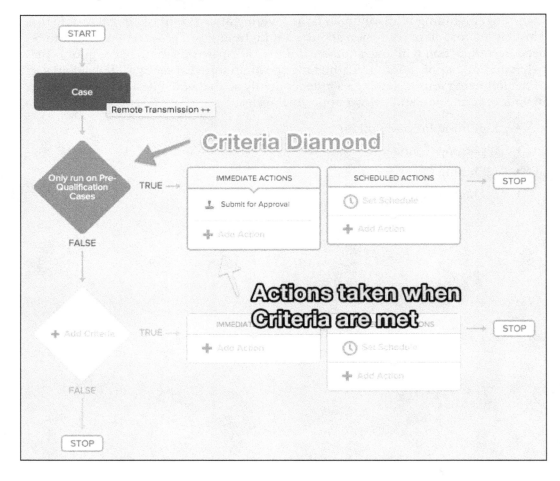

As you can imagine, diagrams for more complex processes can be daunting at first glance. However, reading them couldn't be easier. Reading a Process Builder process starts from the upper-left side of the screen. After the **START** icon, the next icon displayed is the object on which this process will act. In our case, the object in the preceding diagram is **Case**. Just like triggers and workflow rules, Process Builder processes are built with a single object in mind. You can define processes on most sObjects, including custom ones. Some objects, like `SaveResult` or `BatchableContext`, are not Process Builder-enabled. After the initial object icon, look for one or more diamonds. Each diamond represents a set of criteria. When those criteria are met, the actions defined in the squares to the right of that diamond are executed. You can define multiple criteria steps; this allows you to define one process that handles many different possible input criteria. For instance, you could have one process on a **Case** with three criteria diamonds matching record types X, Y, or Z; each with their own sets of actions.

There are two types of action that can be taken: immediate actions and scheduled actions. Scheduled actions allow you to schedule some bit of work for the future. For instance, you can create a process on a **Case** that sends a follow-up e-mail to the client 10 days after the case is created. Or, you might create a series of onboarding e-mails, each firing one day after the previous for the first 5 days after a contact is created. It's worth noting that due to UI constraints, only the first couple of immediate or scheduled actions are listed. Rest assured that the rest of your actions are present, but they are hidden behind the **more actions** text.

Perhaps the single most powerful feature of Process Builder is its ability to be extended with custom Apex code. Writing Apex classes with methods conforming to and using the `@invocableMethod` annotation allows you, the developer, to create custom actions that your administrators can use over and over without your involvement. Additionally, this allows your administrators to modify the conditions that records must meet before the action is run without developers having to rewrite the class or trigger code. This means many, if not the vast majority of triggers can actually be developed as processes and a few custom Process Builder actions.

The @InvocableActions interface

Invocable actions are methods annotated with @invocableAction. This annotation accepts two named parameters: Label and Description. Label is the word or phrase the process builder will associate with your method. Description is the friendly **what does this do** text that appears in the Process Builder alongside the label.

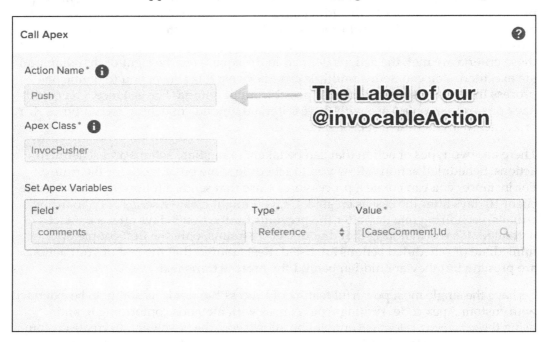

In practice, this looks as follows:

```
Public class myInvocableAction {
@invocableAction(label='BestActionEver' description='Seriously, it's
the best action ever')
  public void bestActionEver(List<Account> accountsOfDoom){
    // do stuff
  }
}
```

As an astute reader, you've no doubt noticed that our method accepted a list of accounts as a parameter. The good news is that invocableAction annotated methods *can* accept a single parameter; the bad news is that there are some constraints. Primitive Objects, such as Integer, String, and Double, concrete sObjects, such as Account, Contact, Opportunity, and custom sObjects, such as MyCustomSObject__c, can all be passed into invocableAction annotated methods. Additionally, Lists, including lists of lists can be passed in, so long as each list contains concrete sObject types. However, lists of generic sObjects (List<sObject>) tag or even the generic Object cannot be passed in.

At first glance, this can seem like an excruciating limitation. After all, if we cannot pass in a generic sObject, we have to duplicate the action for every sObject type in our system. However, there are two methods to overcome this, which should be pointed out. If at all possible, utilize a List<Id> for input. Regardless of the type of object referenced, the ID type will match the reference. This allows you to send multiple object references into the method at once. Note that even though lists are ordered, you should still be using the ID instance method getSObjectType() to verify the IDs passed in. The code looks something like this:

```
Map<Schema.SObjectType,List<Id>> InputObjectsByType = new Map<Schema.
SObjectType,List<Id>>();
For(Id i:InputIds){
  Schema.SObjectType t = i.getSObjectType();
  If(InputObjectsByType.containsKey(t){
    InputObjectsByType.get(t).add(i);
  } else {
    InputObjectsByType.put(t, new List<Id>{i});
  }
}
```

Dropping the input values into a map by their sObjectType tokens allows you to grab objects by their token names, facilitating easy access to multiple kinds of input objects.

If, however, you'd like to avoid doing more SOQL queries, it is possible to construct custom objects annotated with @invocableVariable and utilize these in your InvocableMethod. Like invocableMethods, invocableVariables are created via an Apex annotation, @invocableVariable, that accepts three optional parameters: Label, Description, and Required. The first two function identically to their invocableMethod counterparts. The Required parameter allows you to force a value to be passed in. The invocableVariables object can exist in inner or child classes of a class containing invocableMethods. You can utilize these inner classes as the input type for your invocableMethod method. Consider the following example:

```
public class IM_EasyCalc {

  public class additionInput {
    @invocableVariable(Required = true Label = 'First Number'
      Description = 'First number to add')
    public Integer first;
    @invocableVariable(Required = true Label = 'Second Number'
      Description = 'Second number to add')
    public Integer second;
  }

  public class additionResult {
    @invocableVariable
    public Integer result;
    public AdditionResult(Integer a, Integer b) {
      this.result = a + b;
    }
  }

  @invocableMethod(Label = 'Add' Description = 'Add Two Numbers')
  public static List<AdditionResult>
    addTwoNumbers(List<AdditionInput> requests) {
    List<AdditionResult> results = new List<AdditionResult>();
    for (AdditionInput request : requests) {
      results.add(new AdditionResult(request.first,
        request.second));
    }
    return results;
  }
}
```

In this case, we're using an inner class `AdditionInput` as the list type for the `invocableMethod` input. In Process Builder, this allows us to dictate the input for the type that is passed in. While our `invocableAction` method can only accept a single parameter, parameter that can be a list of custom classes whose inputs are set by the Process Builder selected by the admin! The output of the preceding code will be as shown in the following screenshot:

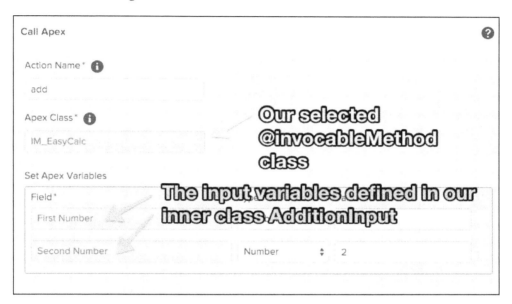

Other caveats

Invocable actions are called via the REST API, and this is both a blessing and a curse. Because they are invoked as API calls, each Invocable action executes in its own Apex transaction, meaning that your code isn't competing for the same CPU governor limit time as other triggers or managed package code. On the other hand, it does utilize REST API calls, which are governed on a 24-hour rotating basis. Heavily executed processes may incur significant API usage; which developers must be aware of. Additionally, there are a few caveats around the actual `invocableMethod` annotation. Only one method in any given class can be annotated as `invocableMethod`. Because of this, you should utilize a consistent naming convention that clearly indicates which classes only exist to wrap the singular `invocableMethod`. For instance, I use `IM_ActionName`. Furthermore, you need to establish an architecture consisting of libraries and objects that contain small but efficient methods that can be composed together with other methods to facilitate complex logic.

Finally, Invocable actions can not only receive a singular input parameter, but they can also return a value to the process. This value must be a list, however, and cannot contain generic sObjects or its primitive cousin object. Any other user-defined sObject, standard Object, or primitive is allowed. While the action can return a value, using the returned value is not entirely intuitive. In order to utilize return values, you have to call the invocableMethod from Flow, not from process. The good news is you can trigger a UI-less flow directly from the Process Builder by selecting an action type Flows. This allows you to select any predefined autolaunched or headless flow that you've created.

Process Builder wrap up

Process builder allows administrators and nondevelopers to not only execute workflow style actions but also call Apex code and flows without ever developing a single line of code. Additionally, Process Builder processes can be modified without changing the code. Administrators can call Apex methods directly by choosing the Apex action type; or for more complex logic, administrators can start autolaunched or headless flows that can utilize values returned by InvocableMethod annotated methods. Developers writing InvocableMethods should keep in mind two key things. First, the process or flow calling the InvocableMethod, and not the InvocableMethod itself, is responsible for determining whether or not the action should run. Secondly, while InvocableMethods can accept only a single input parameter, that input parameter can be a list of a custom type defined by variables that are annotated as @invocableVariable, some or all of which can be defined as required.

Lightning Connect

Lightning Connect is, like much of the lightning suite, actually a group of closely related tools used to accomplish a singular goal. In the case of Lightning Connect, the goal is to surface data residing in external data stores inside Salesforce. This is accomplished by securely exposing data through the oData protocol. The oData protocol is an OASIS standard for REST APIs and data interchange. Through oData endpoints, data can be exposed from common database systems, data science tools, and software libraries. Implementations exist for Microsoft SQL server, PostgreSQL, MySQL, SAP and many other common business systems. Additionally, many common development platforms can also act as oData providers with libraries existing for Rails, Django, and .Net.

Once the data store is `oData` enabled, administrators can establish **external objects**. These external objects provide on-the-fly access to your data via `oData`. From a user perspective, they're virtually identical to standard custom objects with a few restrictions. Unlike standard custom objects, they end not in __c but __x. As you can imagine, certain features of the Salesforce platform are not available with external objects. Most of these stem from the external objects' read-only nature. Features such as sharing, triggers, field history tracking, and processes are not available to external objects. Unintuitively, however, things like merge fields, validation rules, and actions are also not available. While you're not able to create master detail relationships between external objects, you can create lookup relationships to external objects. These are identified as **external lookups** and are set when you create the external object. Often, Salesforce automatically generates these relationships when you establish the `oData` link. In addition to the external lookups between external objects, you can establish an **indirect lookup** between standard or custom sObjects and external objects. This means you can display related external objects on, say, the account detail page.

Combined together, `oData` providers and external objects allow you to access data from external stores without having to import that data into Salesforce. Using this data access allows you to report on and combine on-premises data with salesforce data seamlessly. This can be done not only with built-in reporting tools but also with SOQL. Accessing external objects in SOQL is as simple as querying the __x representation of the object. `SELECT ExternalID FROM orders__x`, for instance, is a perfectly valid query. Running this query causes Salesforce to access the remote data store via `oData`. This does result in a slightly longer query execution time.

Limitations

Lightning Connect is conceptually very easy to understand, but this is deceptive. Accessing external data inside Salesforce has been the goal of countless custom integrations over the years. What makes Lightning Connect different, however, is its ease of use. Point-and-click tools to establish such integrations is what sets Lightning Connect apart. Unfortunately, the point-and-click nature of Lightning Connect's magic extends only so far; and like all great products version one has several limitations and assumptions baked in. Chief amongst the limitations of Lightning Connect is that it's *currently read-only*. While you can easily surface data inside Salesforce with Lightning Connect, you cannot modify it and save it back to the external data source. Future versions of `oData` may support read-write data connections, but as application architects, it may not always be in our best interest to establish such read-write connections.

Like many other features of the Force.com platform, there are governor limits in place to ensure that no one org is able to destabilize the multitenant environment. Most of the governor limits around Lightning Connect are focused on the amount of data passed around. For instance, there is a maximum request size of 8 MB limiting the amount of data each query can return. Other limits are focused on usage. For instance, there are governor limits related to the number of queries you can make in a given hour. For the Enterprise edition and above, it's 10,000 queries an hour, and for developer edition orgs, you can build out and test Lightning Connect with 1,000 requests an hour. Interestingly, these query limits can be disabled, albeit with some tradeoffs. If you designate an external data source as high data volume, you can avoid most of the rate limits at the expense of having these objects available to you in Salesforce1 and Chatter. If your use case is hitting rate limits and you don't need access to your external objects in Salesforce1 or Chatter, this is a viable option. Governor limits for Lightning Connect are listed partially here, but the full list of governor limits can be found on the success community:

General Lightning Connect Limits

For each user, the maximum number of external objects to which you may grant object permissions is equal to the maximum number of custom objects that the user is allowed to access. This limit is determined by the user license that's assigned to the user.

Maximum external objects per organization[1]	100
Maximum joins per query across external objects and other types of objects	4
Maximum length of the OAuth token that's issued by the external system	1,020 characters

[1] The limit of 100 external objects applies regardless of how many Lightning Connect add-ons you purchase for your organization.

The following limits apply only to the OData 2.0 adapter for Lightning Connect.

Maximum HTTP request size for OData	8 MB
Maximum HTTP response size for OData	8 MB
Maximum result set size for an OData query	16 MB
Maximum result set size for an OData subquery	1,000 rows
Maximum new rows retrieved per hour per external data source	50,000

(This limit doesn't apply to high-data-volume external data sources or to rows that have previously been retrieved.)

An organization is limited to:

- 10,000 OData queries per hour for Enterprise, Performance, and Unlimited Editions. Higher limits are available on request.
- 1,000 OData queries per hour for Developer Edition.

Example use cases

If your company uses SAP as the system of record for orders and manufacturing, but uses Salesforce for sales, support, and community management, it's likely beneficial to know what a customer may have ordered in the past inside Salesforce. Surfacing that SAP data via Lightning Connect can help support quickly determine whether a malfunctioning part was in the same batch as similar support calls. In such a situation, the support team identifies a trend of failing parts across multiple clients. Support would have the ability to run a report using standard reporting tools to identify other clients who have parts from the bad batch, but they wouldn't be able to write data back to SAP about which clients were affected.

Lightning Components

Lightning Components are a new UI framework for developing rich applications that are seamlessly mobile. Lightning Components, as their name suggests, are components, or building blocks for developing applications. Lightning is built on top of the open source Aura JavaScript application development framework. You can read more about the Aura open source project at `https://github.com/forcedotcom/aura`. Aura is event driven, and as a result, so are lightning components. Whenever you are working with components, you'll often run into tags that start with Aura. For instance, when you create a new component, the system will scaffold out the bare minimum component needed to work, something like this:

```
<aura:component>
  <!-- your component details here -->
</aura:component>
```

Aura components are actually bundles of many different files separated nicely by concern. Not all of the files need to be populated; for instance, the renderer file isn't required. In the following screenshot, you can see the COMPONENT file open with the initial scaffold data in place. Note that while we are using the developer console in our screenshots, components are one area of Salesforce development where the developer console is the best of breed tool. There are plugins for Sublime and Eclipse, but by far the best experience is found with the developer console.

Aura and, as a result, Lightning Components utilize attributes and expressions for holding and manipulating data. In this component fragment, for example, we establish a string attribute:

```
<Aura:Component>
  <Aura:Attribute Name="ClientName" Type="String" Default="Marc
    Benioff"/>
</Aura:Component>
```

This attribute and its value can be accessed using the v object in expressions. These expression objects have single character names and can be a bit confusing. However, essentially they boil down to this:

- v: This stands for the value of attributes
- c: This stands for the controller, though this can refer to the client-side JavaScript controller or the Apex controller attached to the component, or to the component itself
- UI: This stands for the user interface elements

These objects can be accessed within the scope of expressions. These are similar to Visualforce expressions and have a similar syntax. For instance, to use the value of an attribute as the text of a button, you would access it this way:

```
<Aura:Component>
  <Aura:Attribute Name="ClientName" Type="String" Default="Marc
    Benioff"/>
<ui:button label="call {!v.ClientName}" press="{!c.MakeCall}"/>
</Aura:Component>
```

Here, we added a single line of code that has two expressions in it—one a reference to the value of the ClientName attribute and another to call the MakeCall method on the controller. Here is a screenshot as an example:

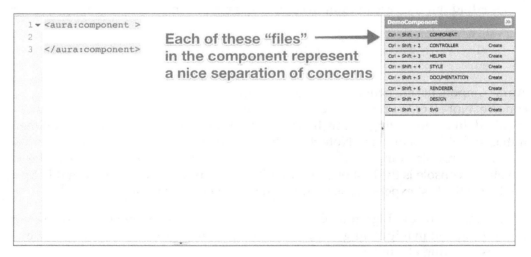

Clicking on the **CONTROLLER** option on the right or using the *Ctrl + Shift + 2* key combo will open up the `javascript` controller file, as shown in the following screenshot. It's not entirely intuitive what these files do by name, so here's a breakdown:

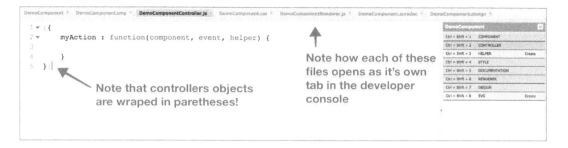

Component files

The COMPONENT file is used for the markup of the component setting up the core UI of your component. If your component needs a pick list, for instance, the component file is where you place the `<select>` tags.

The CONTROLLER file is where your JavaScript controller lives. This controller encapsulates the actions and logic your component uses. The standard interface for a Lightning Component controller is as shown here:

```
({
   customAction : function(comp, evt, helper) {
      //Your custom logic here
   }
})
```

As intercomponent communication occurs by firing events, your controller methods are often event handlers or event emitters. Emitter methods take the following general form and utilize the `.fire()` method to fire off the event:

```
customEmitter : function(cmp, event, helper) {
var myObj = cmp.get("v.myObj");
var myEvent = $A.get("e.namespace:someEvent");
myEvent.setParams({ "myObj": myObj}).fire();
}
```

Note the use of the $A global variable. This is your access to the Aura object. It provides a number of utility and access methods including the `.get()` method, which functions similarly to the jQuery selector system. Using `get` you can access application wide events.

The HELPER file exists to contain helper methods that can be reused in multiple places throughout the component. Specifically, it helps you write logic that is passed by reference to both controllers and renderers. This allows you to keep your renderers and controllers relatively clean, easy to read, and minimizes duplicate logic. For instance, if you have code that calls back to an Apex controller and you need to access it from both your controller and renderer, you can place that code inside the helper and reference it from both using helper.commonMethod:

```
// Your controller
callApexController: function(cmp, helper) {
  helper.hCallApexController ();
}

// Your renderer
afterRender: function(cmp, helper) {
    this.superAfterRender();
    helper.hCallApexController ();
}

// Your helper
hCallApexController: function(cmp, helper) {
var a = component.get("c.getS1Data");
a.setCallback(this, function(action) {
if (a.getState() === "SUCCESS") {
   //handle the data returned
} else {
//handle the error
}
});

    $A.enqueueAction(a);
}
```

In the preceding example, we extracted the logic for calling an Apex controller method and handling the results to the helper file. We can use that logic easily by calling helper.hCallApexController(). Aside from promoting reusability, this helps us ensure that when we fix bugs related to our Apex callout, there is only one place to fix them! Also, take note of the naming convention I used for the helper method. You don't have to preface your helper methods with h but adopting a logical and consistent naming convention allows your teammates and your future self to easily know that this method is not defined later in the controller, but in the helper file.

In our preceding example code, you saw references to both a controller and a renderer. We have not discussed renderers yet because you don't need to worry about creating a customer renderer generally. In fact, you only need to create or edit the renderer if you need to modify the way the standard renderer works. When overriding or customizing the renderer, ensure that you always call `this.superRender();` first. Once you've done that, you can include custom logic or even call `helper` methods like the example does.

Renderers provide a place for you to override the standard render methods. This allows you to, for instance, trigger logic when a particular render method runs. For instance, look at this simple re-render override:

```
rerender : function(cmp, helper){
    this.superRerender();
    helper.disableSubmitButton(cmp);
}
```

In this case, the component that will fire `rerender` automatically whenever a component attribute is modified will fire this custom version, rather than the default `rerender` method. Our custom `rerender` method does two things. First, it calls the main `rerender` method, as triggered by `this.superRerender();` and then calls our `helper.disableSubmitButton();` method. This effectively allows us to call custom logic (in this case, our `disableSubmitButton` logic), whenever one of the standard render methods is called (in this case, the `rerender` method). Disabling a **submit** button or other UI-based properties is perfect for this sort of automatically chained logic.

So when do you need your own render object? You'll need a custom renderer if, for example, you want to update a component whenever a second component is changed. In that case, your second component's renderer would call a `helper` method to update the first component.

The STLYE file contains all the CSS needed to style your component as you see fit. This is, perhaps, the most straightforward of the component's files. There is really only one thing that differentiates this CSS file from the numerous others you've worked on in the past. The scaffolding for the `style` file is as follows:

```
.THIS {
}
```

The .THIS tag is the essential difference. When your component is utilized, the framework dynamically replaces the .THIS element with the component's instance name. This allows you to override styles for your component without stepping on another component's identically named .awesomeDiv style. In other words, if you have two instances of a custom button component, the framework will automatically replace the .THIS element with the instance name of each component. That way, the styling of one instance won't interfere or overwrite the styling of the second instance. For example, if you programmatically change one component's .THIS styling, the second instance of that component is not affected!

The DOCUMENTATION file is where all of the utilization documentation for your component goes. While this is, I believe, primarily for components based on AppExchange to write packaged documentation for their components, as application developers, we should never forget to take every opportunity to document design decisions, tradeoffs, and assumptions. Eventually, even the most well-written software exhibits bugs, and the better written code is, the harder it can be to decipher after months or years of writing it. Use the documentation file to help your future self and your team! Also note, that you can access the full documentation of your org's Lightning components by visiting the auradocs application in your org—AuraDocs at https://<Instance> lightning.force.com/auradocs. Keep in mind, however, that if you've not written documentation for your custom components, it won't be visible in the auradocs app.

The DESIGN file can be a bit hard to understand. In a way, it's a header file for your component. Like C header files, the design file describes the methods, attributes, and events your component exposes so that the Lightning App Builder and other visual tools can properly guide the user in using your component. For instance, you might expose an attribute in a design file like this:

```
<design:component>
    <design:attribute name="Customer" label="Customer"
description="Customer contact Id you wish to interact with" />
</design:component>
```

In this design file, we enabled a single attribute named Customer. This will be displayed in the Lightning App Builder with the **Customer** label and the description will be **Customer Contact ID you wish to interact with**. These label and description parameters help end users who are creating applications with your components to see what data to pass in.

Lastly, but certainly important is the svg file. This file contains the SVG data of your **components** icon. Even if you are not developing your component for distribution, you should provide an icon to help distinguish it from other components in the Lightning App Builder.

@auraEnabled Apex

As mentioned earlier, you can call the Apex controller methods from within your Lightning Component. This is one of the features that Lightning adds to the Aura project. To make such calls, however, you have to annotate your controller methods with the @auraEnabled tag. Here's an example:

```
public class LAccountController {
    @AuraEnabled
    public static List<Account> getAccountsWithBillingAddress() {
        return [SELECT Name, Id, BillingAddress FROM Account Order
By Id Limit 20];
    }
}
```

Here, our Apex controller exposes only a single method, but since it is @auraEnabled, we can call it from our Lightning Component. However, we'll need to associate the controller and the component together by modifying our component markup to include the controller, as follows:

```
<aura:component controller="Namesapce.LAccountController">
 <!-- component details -->
</aura:component>
```

Note the additional controller attribute on the first line. This associates the component with the LAccountController controller found in the Namespace namespace. One of the things you have to do to start with Lighting Component development is define a namespace for your org. If you select CompanyName as your namespace, your invocation of the controller would read CompanyName.LAccountController. When your component is initialized, it will have access to the @auraEnabled methods in your Apex controller. It should also be noted that any Apex class will have to be tested to the same standards as non AuraEnabled classes are.

Lightning future

Lightning is, I believe, the future of UI and custom app development on the Salesforce platform. It's write-once, run on all screen sizes feature set means that any app is mobile by default. That said, I don't think `Visualforce` is going away any time soon. Lightning is the future, but not the exclusive future. One reason I believe Lightning is the future stems from Salesforce's tireless march to make development of business applications easier, and, well, less developer focused. Lighting Process Builder, for instance, enables admins to create complex logic without writing a single line of code. Developers who write code are still needed to develop actions and write components, but the shift isn't about eliminating developers. Indeed, the shift is in enabling more people to develop more apps faster by relying on off-the-shelf actions and components. Nowhere is this shift more easily seen than in the final feature of Lightning—the Lightning App Builder.

Lightning App Builder

Lightning App Builder is an integrated development environment for people who don't write code. Instead, the idea is to present a user with data and prebuilt off-the-shelf components that play well together. If you'd like to give it a spin, you can access the Lightning App Builder in any Summer '15 or newer org by clicking on **Lightning App Builder** under the **Create** submenu in **Setup**. The first step in creating a new Lightning App is to choose the template. Note the new column layouts, **2** and **3**, that are available here:

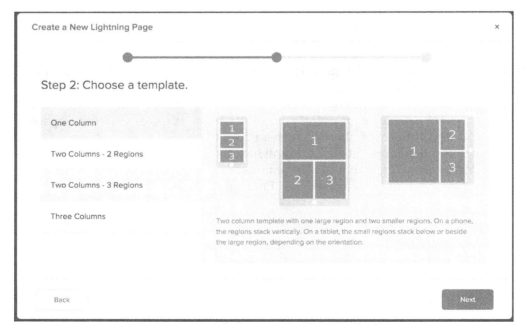

Having selected a template, developers are taken to the App Builder Canvas, which looks like this:

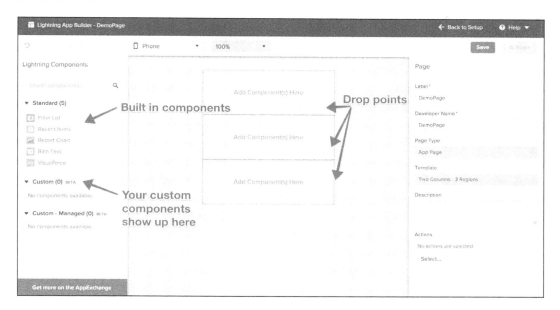

The palette to the left shows a list of components available to the developer. Split into three segments, the first shows all of the built-in components, such as **Filter List**, recently used items, and **Visualforce**. After this, there are two groups of components. The first section display custom developed components and components available via AppExchange Packages. Beware, however, that your component must have the `implements="flexipage:availableForAllPageTypes"` component attribute in order to be used in the App Builder. Additionally, only components that have design files will show up in App Builder. Code developers can create custom components, package them, and distribute them through the AppExchange. Developers using the Lightning App Builder who have installed that app exchange package would see those components in the final section.

The center section displays the application's UI as you create it. Simply drag and drop options from the left palette to the drop points labeled **Add Component(s) Here**. This is the prime example of the shift away from traditional app development to lightning. It's easy and incredibly fast to drag and drop a few components onto an app canvas; much faster than writing Visualforce pages, controllers, and tests. By relying on prebuilt components that play nicely with each other, development of business process apps has never been faster.

Finally, the palette to the right holds the details of the currently selected object. If we were to drag a filtered list to the top most component's drop point and highlight it, the right palette would display the details of our filtered list component:

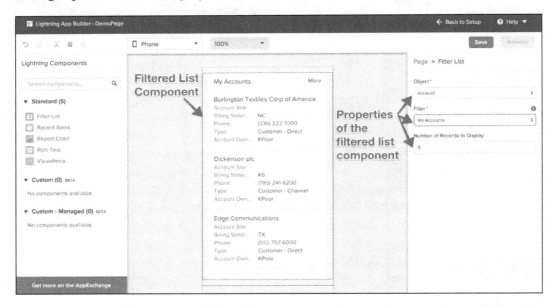

These properties are the attributes of the component exposed through the design file, which we discussed earlier. The SVG file of the component is used as the icon in the left palette.

In our previous screenshots, we previewed with a phone-sized screen, but by selecting a tablet or desktop view from the drop-down menu at the top of the center pane, you can preview other sizes as well. Here's what our app would look like if you added a report chart and viewed it as a tablet app:

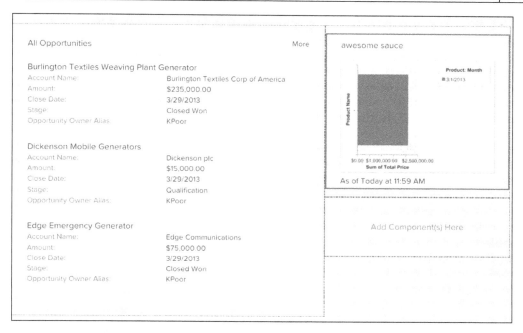

The double-edged sword of Lightning App Builder is that your functionality is largely confined to the components that are available. While it's true, that you can include Visualforce pages; they have to be self-contained to be functional. For instance, including a Visualforce page that requires a URL parameter of Id to be populated results in this error when you add it as a component:

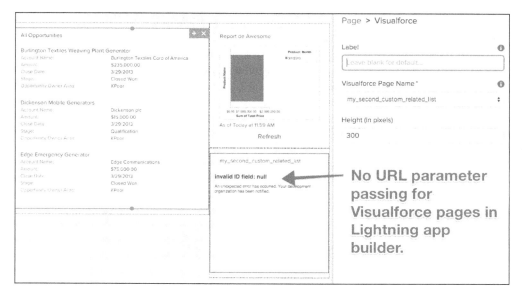

Of course, as coding developers, we can easily write custom components to add functionality and features to our Lightning apps. I imagine there will be a healthy set of AppExchange components available sooner rather than later. In the meantime, Lightning App Builder is a fantastic replacement for current dashboards! Offering different and expanded layouts with the ability to include charts from reports as well as related lists built by custom filters, there's quite a few compelling reasons to build dashboards in the Lightning app builder, with just the built-in components!

This chapter serves as an overview of the various concepts and features of Lightning. Lightning, however, is an evolving product with new and refined features in every release. Because of this, I encourage you to read through the lightning section of each set of release notes that Salesforce puts out. While features such as the Lightning Process builder are unlikely to disappear, they may very well change. For instance, I wouldn't be surprised if at some point, Process builder became bulk enabled. Likewise, I expect the Lightning app builder to have an ever increasing set of components available to developers. Lightning Connect may one day be able to write data back to the external data source. Time will tell, but even with these features and tools where they are today, they represent a powerful shift in what it means to develop business applications. Instead of writing countless triggers, coding developers are empowered to develop cutting edge components and actions for non-coding developers to rapidly drag and drop into place for graphically stunning apps that can easily adapt to changing business rules.

Summary

In this chapter, we scratched the surface of the four lightning features—Lightning Process Builder, Lightning Connect, Lightning Components, and the Lightning App Builder. In the next few years, I expect Lightning Components and the Lightning App Builder will start replacing the venerable Visualforce for custom UIs on the platform. Until then, Process Builder remains a fantastically powerful addition to the platform that can even replace basic triggers. Lightning Connect, on the other hand, has immediate benefits for accessing data stored outside the platform.

In our next chapter, we'll start getting into the thick of unit testing, discussing how, why, and what to test!

5
Writing Efficient and Useful Unit Tests

Unit testing is the single most important skill an application developer can master. Sadly, writing unit tests is rarely seen as exciting, let alone important. This chapter will focus on testing various Apex components. We will discuss what to test, when to write the tests, and most importantly, how to test. We will cover the following topics:

- Why do we write unit tests?
- What to test—discussing positive, negative, and role-based testing
- When do we write unit tests?
- How do we structure tests for speed and code reuse?
- Mocking
- Tips and tricks for efficient testing

Why do we write unit tests?

Often, it seems that the answer to why do we write unit tests is because Salesforce makes us do it! This, however, is not the reason we should be writing unit tests. All classes in production orgs have to have 75% code coverage and all triggers must have some coverage. Salesforce enforces this for a number of reasons. As the platform evolves and new features are added, Salesforce needs to ensure that your applications will continue to run without an issue. To do this, they employ the **hammer**, a specialized test harness that allows them to run every unit test in every org twice. First, the hammer runs every test in every org on the current version of the platform. These same tests are then run on the pre-release version of the platform. This helps them ensure that your code not only runs on the new version of the platform, but that it also runs at least as efficiently as it did on the earlier platforms. Even if your unit tests have no assertions and utterly fail to do anything but run code, the hammer's execution of your tests provides valuable insight into the backward compatibility and efficiency of the platform. This illustrates an important point. Contrary to popular belief, the true cost of software is not in development but in maintenance. The Apex software on the Salesforce1 platform is no exception. While there are upfront development costs, the true cost of the software adds up as after months and years after the initial implementation, developers try to add features, fix bugs, or change the implementation of objects and functions. Without hammer and the unit tests it runs, the cost of upgrading the Salesforce platform would be astronomical! Not only for Salesforce, but for every client running code on the platform. With that in mind, let's look at some concrete positive reasons for writing unit tests.

Proving functionality

The classic reason for unit testing is to prove that the code works as you believe it does. Given an addition method accepting two integer numbers we can assert the output of the method when we know the input. Proving the functionality of our code is the foundation of our testing philosophy because it gives us assurance not only that our code's architecture, engineering, and logic are correct, but also that we understand how that code interacts within the greater system.

Reducing the cost of change

As a system evolves, features are added, deprecated, and changed. It's relatively easy for knowledgeable developers to add features. However, it's difficult to safely deprecate features. The highest risk to a system, however, comes from changing the implementation of the given features. This is where unit tests can save vast amounts of time. Imagine being tasked with replacing the implementation of a complex `calculateIncomeTax` method. The current implementation and the new implementation are functionally identical, but your new method is 5x faster. Because both implementations are expected to function identically existing tests are valid proofs of functionality for both implementations. Because of this, replacing the implementation of a complex method becomes safer and easier. Make a change to the implementation, and so long as the tests pass, you can be confident you've not introduced a bug.

Encouraging modular, reusable code

As you start to write unit tests for your code, you'll quickly learn that poorly designed, tightly coupled code is difficult to test. Writing tests to ensure software quality and maintainability, rather than to meet deployment requirements, will force certain design choices on your code. You'll end up with code that is more loosely coupled, with less reliance on state, and is generally simpler. Such code is easier to test, and is therefore easier to functionally prove. Additionally, because it no longer requires maintaining state or tightly coupled relationships with other objects, this type of code is almost always reusable code, which is never a bad thing.

Identifying engineering bugs you didn't write

If you're writing software for a living, you're working to solve complex real-world problems, not to prove your understanding of computer science principles. The situations and problems you're tasked with solving are not simple problems, but nuanced, intricate problems complex enough to justify custom software. This can lead to seemingly crazy bugs that are incredibly hard to solve. There are situations where your code fails because of some other bit of code that fails only on the last day of the month or at midnight on Thursdays. I call these *Cinderella* bugs because they only happen at midnight on the night of the ball. Writing unit tests help you identify these situations before you experience them in production. Granted, you'll need to show some creativity when writing your tests, but learning to test your billing code at midnight on Thursdays is generally the kind of lesson you only need to learn once.

Documenting expected behavior

It's a truism that the job you have now is likely not your first, nor your last. Inevitably we will face the daunting task of learning a new code base. On top of that, outside of a computer science textbook, when have any of us ever encountered a code base that consistently followed best practices as well as proper and sensible object oriented abstractions? Indeed. When I was working as a consultant, coming up to speed on a org's code base was a weekly chore. One of the best ways I've ever found to get up to speed is to read through the tests. Well written tests demonstrate not only what the code does but also what kinds of data are expected and required for that code to run. Fantastic tests will even walk you through failure scenarios and their causes. Even badly written tests give insight into what the developer was thinking the code should do.

Tests + code = less likely to produce bugs

Even if you only write basic unit tests to prove your code functions as you expect, you've decreased the chances of having bugs in your code. Why? There are a few reasons, but the basic principle is that you're less likely to make a logic mistake in two places than you are in one place. With each test you write, you're decreasing the risk that you've got a logic bug somewhere in the code you are testing. Writing good tests helps by not only exercising your code, but also by helping you think through your code's interaction with the greater system. This is especially true if you write your test code first! Forcing yourself and your team to design new functionality up front causes you to pause and consider what existing code you can reuse as well as consider the impact this functionality has on the greater system.

What not to test?

I'm often asked by developers who are new to the platform what kinds of thing they should write unit tests for. In general, I find that question rather frustrating. Many factors go into answering that question, and without knowing the specifics of your org, it's impossible to answer comprehensively. On the other hand, it's much easier to answer the question what not to test? While the answer to that question isn't cut and dry either, it's at least simpler to provide guidelines for. With that in mind, here are some things you should most likely not test.

Managed package code

Managed packages have to provide their own unit tests. Additionally, you don't get to see the code from managed packages, so writing unit tests for managed package code is not only difficult, it's fruitlessly redundant as well. However, this isn't carte blanche for not testing your code that interacts with the managed package code. The only time I write unit tests for managed package code, is when I'm documenting a bug in that managed package!

Standard platform features

I know this one seems obvious, but I've come across it numerous times. There's nothing to be gained from testing the basic constructs of the Apex language or built-in system-defined classes and functions. It is possible to test whether or not `if()` works, but what's the point? What you want to be testing isn't `if()` but the logical tests that go into that `if()` statement. Also in this category, we have declarative features, such as rollup summary fields, formulas, and validation rules. We write unit tests in part to prove functionality, but we need not write tests to prove platform functionality.

Aside from testing managed package code and standard platform features, the answer to what to test is *everything*, unless it doesn't make sense Testing, just like software development, requires judgment calls, and if something doesn't seem like it makes sense to test, it probably doesn't. However, you should always maintain the posture of testing everything and ruling out only what clearly doesn't make sense.

When to write unit tests

Adherents of test-driven development argue for writing the tests first. Indeed, the idea behind test-driven development is that tests define acceptance of code. In general, the **Test-driven development (TDD)** approach is to write a test, see it fail, and then write just enough code to make the test pass. In practice, this is easier said than done. Others argue that you should write your code and then the tests because it's more efficient. I find the most successful developers almost always develop the code and the tests simultaneously, the code influencing the tests and the tests ensuring that the code is written in a maintainable, testable way. So long as the tests are written, and written well, I find it hard to argue for or against writing the tests first. Indeed, I find it most flexible to write the tests at the same time as the code. The central question of unit testing your code isn't when to test or what to test, but how to test.

Structuring unit tests

In general, there is only one overarching pattern for unit testing code on the Salesforce1 platform. The essential differences between the Salesforce1 platform and other software development stacks does make unit testing is a bit different. That said, if you're familiar with unit testing in other languages, this will largely seem familiar to you. Here's the general pattern:

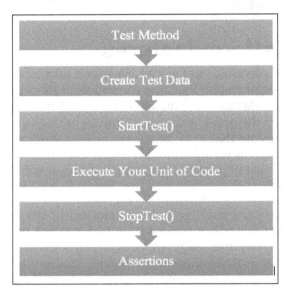

Using your own data

Each of our test methods needs to create its own test data. While this seems cumbersome and time consuming, it's the only safe way to run unit tests. Relying on existing data in your org is problematic because you cannot ensure that the data will exist in your other orgs. Assuming an account will exist in your production org just because it exists in your development sandbox is a great recipe for frustrating deployments. This often finds its way into our tests through the use of hardcoded IDs. Querying for an account where the ID is X, for instance, not only assumes that the account exists in other orgs, but also that its fields contain the same values, including the ID field.

While creating your own test data can seem cumbersome and time consuming, there are a couple of things you can do to help with that. First and foremost, use a test factory. Test factories provide easy-to-remember methods for generating your test data. Additionally, they reflect the metadata of your org at runtime, allowing the test factory to dynamically know which fields are required and how to populate them intelligently. While there are a number of test factory libraries available, I'm a fan of Daniel Hoechst's Salesforce `Test-Factory`, which you can find on GitHub at `https://github.com/dhoechst/Salesforce-Test-Factory`. With his test factory in place, generating your own data for your tests is as simple as a call, like this:

```
// Calling TestFactory will pre-fill all the fields we need
Account a = (Account)TestFactory.createSObject(new Account());
insert a;

// You can also manually set specific values to be used.
// Any values set in the constructor will override the defaults
Opportunity o = (Opportunity)TestFactory.createSObject(new
Opportunity(AccountId = a.Id));

// You can also specify a specific set of overrides for different
scenarios
Account a = (Account)TestFactory.createSObject(new Account(),
'TestFactory.AccountDefaults');

// Finally, get a bunch of records for testing bulk
Account[] aList = (Account[])TestFactory.createSObjectList(new
Account(), 200);

// You can optionally insert records as created like this:
// Note the final parameter of true.
Account a = (Account) TestFactory.createSObject(new Account(), true);
Contact c = (Contact) TestFactory.createSObject(new Contact(AccountID
= a.Id), true);
```

Even with a test factory in place, it can be cumbersome to have twenty lines of code in each test simply setting up data. Here's where the second tip comes into play. While the test factory can provide specific sObjects for us, we often need a collection of related objects to test with. For instance, we may need an opportunity with opportunity line items associated with it for our test. Normally, that would require creating not just the opportunity and opportunity line items but also the account and any contacts we may need. In these situations, it makes sense to establish one or more customized test factories that rely on and build on the functionality of the basic test factory. I like to ensure that everything is easy to find, so I tend to have many sObject specific test factories. Consider the following instance:

```
@isTest
Public Without Sharing Class OpportunityTestFactory {

   Public Static genOppWithLineItemsAndAccount(Integer
     numLineItems, Boolean doInsert){
     Account a = (Account)TestFactory.createSObject(New Account(),
       doInsert);
     Opportunity o = (Opportunity)TestFactory.createSObject(New
       Opportunity(accountId=a.id), doInsert);
     List<OpportunityLineItem> olis = new
       List<OpportunityLineItem>();
     for(Integer i = 0; i < numLineItems; i++) {
       olis.add((OpportunityLineItem)TestFactory.createSObject(new
         OpportunityLineItem(OpportunityId=o.id)));
     }
     if(doInsert){
       insert olis;
     }
     return o;
   }
}
```

These kinds of customized test factories grow over time but having them means it's easy to add additional custom methods and easier to write tests using your own data. Two tips on custom test factories. First, always annotate them as @isTest at the class level. This ensures that the code cannot be called in a non-test environment and that it doesn't count against your overall code coverage. Secondly, note how I've maintained the optional insert flag for the method in the preceding code. If your test doesn't rely on triggers and other **data manipulation language (DML)** based operations, you can often write faster running tests by not inserting or querying. Oftentimes, however, you will have to insert the data, and maintaining that simple Boolean flag in your custom factory methods makes it that much easier to do.

Starting and stopping your tests

One of the unique features of the Salesforce1 platform is its governor limits. These limits are intended to keep you from writing inefficient code and, more importantly, ensure that no one org is using vast amounts of resources at the detriment of other org's. Having said that, they can often cause problems when writing tests. After all, if you're creating your own test data, and testing in bulk, you may very well run into the max DML or max query count limits. This is why Salesforce created the platform-unique `startTest` and `stopTest` methods. These methods do more than just delineating the portions of your test that exercise your code; they provide you with two invaluable services. First, calling `startTest()` will reset your governor limits and limit them to just the code between `startTest()` and `stopTest()`. This means that you are free to create your test data without the creation of that data causing you to hit a governor limit. Additionally, it means that when the test runs, the governor limits summary at the end of the log is a summary not of the test itself, but of your tested code. This is incredibly useful for identifying processes and methods that, for instance, sometimes hit the execution time limit.

Secondly, calling `stopTest()` forces all asynchronous code to complete before returning to the test. This is invaluable as you write asynchronous code, such as `@future` methods and queueable Apex. This means that `stopTest()` will force any asynchronous work to complete not at some point in the future, but right now so that you can continue to test. This allows you to follow the same pattern for testing regardless of the tested code's synchronicity.

Executing your code

After creating test data and calling `test.startTest()`, we are now left with executing our code. This is where our general testing pattern branches into three subpatterns. Each of these subpatterns does execute the code, but each in their own unique and important way. Of the three, the first subpattern is the easiest to understand and what you're most likely to have run across. I call this types of tests *Positive tests* because they're based in the positive assumption that your code is working as intended with valid data. The second subpattern is less intuitive, but far more powerful. I call these *Negative tests* because they test what happens when exceptions occur. Lastly, there are *Permissions tests* that test how your code functions with different users, roles, and permission sets. Let's take a more detailed look at all three.

Positive tests

Positive tests prove expected behavior. That is, they prove that the code functions as it is intended to when given valid input. Succinctly stated, this subpattern states that when given proper inputs, expected outputs are received. Care should be taken to evaluate all valid paths through the code. If your code is structured with conditional logic statements, ensure that you positively test each and every viable path through your code. Let's take a look at some class code and it's test to illustrate this:

```
Public class exampleCode {
  Public Integer add(Integer one, Integer two){
    return one + two;
  }
}


@isTest
private class exampleCode_Tests {
  @isTest static void test_Add_Postive() {
    exampleCode drWho = new exampleCode();
    Test.startTest();
    Integer testValue = drWho.add(5,7);
    Test.stopTest();
     System.assertEquals(12, testValue,
        'Expected 5+7 to equal 12');
  }
```

Our simple add() method accepts two integer arguments and returns a single integer in response. Our test follows our basic test pattern, but the simple nature of this method means we don't need to create our own test data here; we can just pass in two integers. You'll note, however, that we're creating the ExampleCode object before we start the test. Because this is a positive test, we'll provide the add method with two valid integers, in this case, 5 and 7. Because we're setting the input parameters, after a couple cups of coffee, we can do the math ourselves and assert that the value returned is 12. This is an extremely simple but clear example of how positive tests work.

Negative tests

Negative tests are less intuitive and require some additional setup. In return, negative tests prove that our code safely handles errors and exceptions. Because we're intentionally providing inputs to the code that will cause an exception to occur, we need to find a way to safely capture the exception without failing the test. Here, the subpattern works by setting a Boolean variable, say `didPass` to `false` in the setup of the test, and executing our to-be-tested code inside a `Try/catch` block. When our inputs cause the test to throw the exception, our test captures that in the `catch` block. If the type of exception and messaging we catch matches what we expect, we can set `didPass` to `true`. Outside of the `Try/catch` block and after the `stopTest()` call, we can assert that our `didPass` variable is `true`. That's a lot to take in, so let's look at the following code example:

```
Public class exampleCode {
  Public class exampleCodeException{}
  Public Static Integer division(Integer one, Integer two){
    if(two == 0) {
      Throw new exampleCodeException('Dividing by zero makes
        kittens cry');
    }
    return one / two;
  }
}

private class exampleCode_Tests {
  @isTest static void test_Divide_Negative() {
    Boolean didCatchProperException = false;
    Test.startTest();
    Try {
      exampleCode.divide(1, 0);
    } catch (exampleCode.exampleCodeException AwesomeException){
      didCatchProperException = true;
    }
    Test.stopTest();
    System.assert(didCatchProperException,
    'Properly caught custom Exception');
  }
```

We've added a division method to our `ExampleCode` class, and astute readers will notice the addition of a new custom exception class, `exampleCodeException`. In our test, we follow the same pattern as earlier of starting the test and executing our code. However, in this situation, we wrap the code execution in a `Try`/`catch` block. We're calling our divide method with an intentionally bad second integer, `0`. Our `divide` method is on the lookout, however, for the second parameter being `0`. Instead of letting the system throw a divide by zero error, our code throws an `ExampleCodeException` method. It's this `exampleCodeException` method that we're trapping in our test's `catch` block. This allows us to be certain that not just any exception is caught here. If, for instance, a divide by zero exception somehow still occurred, that exception would not be caught and the test would fail. In the end, we set `didCatchProperException`, our previously defined test Boolean to `true` so that we can assert that we did indeed catch the proper kind of exception.

Negative tests are considerably more powerful in the long run, helping ensure modifications still properly handle known exception situations properly. This is especially helpful when modifying the implementation of class methods. Additionally, because they're testing how the code reacts to invalid data, they are the de facto way of testing situations, such as invalid user entered data, fields that legitimately have apostrophes in them, and responses to third-party external web services that your code uses. Does your code properly handle the last name `O'Connel`? How about a fellow developer accidently linking a task by `WhatId` instead of `WhoId`? And how does your exchange rate API code handle the sudden lack of Internet connection due to severe weather? Negative tests ensure that you can answer these questions. More importantly, negative tests prove that you've defensively developed against at least those failure scenarios that were identified.

Permissions-based tests

Permissions-based testing ensures that your sharing and security model works as you expect it to. Sharing rules and security options are some of the most complicated aspects of Salesforce1 platform development. These are, therefore, some of the most important tests you can write. But wait you say! Isn't writing tests of the security and permissions model just a form of testing native platform functionality? Kind of. Unless otherwise specified, Apex code runs in a system context. In essence, this means that Apex code normally ignores the users' permissions and sharing rules. These tests help us ensure that the permissions and sharing rules are honored by our Apex code.

Effectively, permission tests follow the same general pattern as other tests with one small twist. When we go to execute the code, we'll execute that code with a different user. We're not just going to pick a user at random either. The user we run the test with becomes a crucial data point that we create. To actually run the test with our newly created user, we call the Salesforce1 platform's `System.runAs()` method. The `RunAs` method accepts a single user parameter and a block. Anything in that block of code is executed as with the profile, role, and permission sets of the user specified. Let's look at a basic use case for `runAs()`:

```
private class exampleCode_Tests {
  @isTest static void test_getBankAccount_AsUserWithTimeLord() {
  User u = UserTestFactory.getUserWithProfile('TimeLord');
  System.runAs(u){
      Test.startTest();
       // This is executed as our user with the Timelord
      // profile
      Test.stopTest();
    }
    // Assertions
}
```

In this test method, we create a user with a call to our `UserTestFactory`. This user is set up with a given profile, in this case, the profile `TimeLord`. This sets us up to test our code as `TimeLord`. Now, when we execute our code, we can ensure that this profile's permissions are honored.

With this subpattern, we can test not only profiles, but also sharing rules and permission sets. Perhaps more importantly, we can test them both positively and negatively! Let's look at some examples. First, let's update our `ExampleCode` class with a method we want to permission test:

```
Public class exampleCode {
  Public class exampleCodeException{}
  Public Integer getBankAccount(Account a){
    // SuperSekr3tBankAccountNum__c is an encrypted field
    a = [SELECT superSekr3tBankAccountNum__c
FROM Account
WHERE ID :a.id];
If(String.ValueOf(a.superSekr3tBankAccountNum__c).contains('*')) {
  Throw new exampleCodeException('Nope!');
}
    return a.SuperSekr3tBankAccountNum__c;
  }
}
```

Here's a positive test:

```
private class exampleCode_Tests {
  @isTest static void test_getBankAccount_Positive() {
    exampleCode drWho = new exampleCode();
    User u = UserTestFactory.getUserWithProfile('TimeLord);
    Account a = (Account)TestFactory.createSObject(new Account());
    Integer result;
    System.runAs(u){
      Test.startTest();
        result = drWho.getBankAccount(a);
      Test.stopTest();
    }
    System.assertNotEquals(result, null,
      'Expected The Doctor to have access to bank #');
  }
}
```

In this test, we expect a user with the TimeLord profile to be able to access the encrypted bank account number field. On the other hand, we want to ensure that other profiles do not have access. With this in mind, we can write a negative test that looks like this:

```
@isTest
private class exampleCode_Tests {
  @isTest static void test_getBankAccount_UberForNope() {
    exampleCode Dalek = new exampleCode();
    User u = UserTestFactory.getUserWithProfile('Dalek');
    Account a = (Account)TestFactory.createSObject(new Account());
    Boolean didCatchException = false;
   Integer result;
    System.runAs(u){
      Test.startTest();
      Try {
          result = Dalek.getBankAccount(a);
      } catch(exampleCode.ExampleCodeException e){
        if(e.getMessage().containsIgnoreCase('nope')){
          didCatchException = true;
        }
      Test.stopTest();
    }
    System.assert(didCatchException, 'Expected Daleks to be blocked');
  }
}
```

Our `getBankAccount()` method queries for an encrypted field; if the user doesn't have permission to view it, it will return a masked value. If we detect that masked value, we throw an exception. Like our positive test, this test still requires a custom user with a given profile, but in this case we expect an exception.

Importantly, we're not limited to testing users with different profiles. We can, and should create tests for Apex-based sharing rules, roles, and permission sets. Permission sets are an incredibly powerful and fine-grained tool for extending permissions on a per-user basis, beyond what a user has from their profile. With permission sets, we can, for instance, establish a singular profile for the entire support staff and grant additional privileges to support managers. If you're not already a fan of permission sets, check them out, you soon will be! Testing permission sets requires just a few extra lines of code to test. This is a prime example, however, of where a custom test factory becomes an invaluable tool. Let's look at some code as another example of testing permission sets:

```
@isTest
private class exampleCode_Tests {
  @isTest static void test_getBankAccount_W_PermSet() {
    exampleCode ClaraOswald = new exampleCode();
    User u = UserTestFactory.getUserWithProfileAndPermSets('Standard
User', new List<String>{'companion'});
    Account a = (Account)TestFactory.createSObject(new Account());
    Boolean result;
    System.runAs(u){
      Test.startTest();
        result = ClaraOswald.getBankAccount(a);
      Test.stopTest();
    }
    System.assertNotEquals(result, null,
  'Expected ClaraOswald who has Companion Permissions to have access
to the bank account');
  }
```

As you can see from the code, our test is nearly identical to our positive profile permission test. In fact, the only difference in this test is the custom `userTestFactory` method we called. Because positive permission tests are so similar, you can often group them together in a data structure. This allows you to write a metatest that iterates over your data structure to test various permissions. This greatly simplifies your testing, allowing you to add an element to your data structure, instead of adding entirely new tests whenever a new permission set or profile is created. Here's how one such meta-test works:

```
@isTest
Public Class accountPermTests {
```

```
   public class PermissionTestData {
      Boolean isProfileTest {get;set;}
      Boolean isPermSetTest {get;set;}
      Boolean isPositiveTest {get;set;}
      String profileName {get;set;}
      String permSetName {get;set;}
      String exceptionTypeName {get;set;}
      String exceptionMessage {get;set;}
      String friendlyMessage {get;set;}
      String assertEqualsValue {get;set;}

      Public PermissionTestData(Boolean iisProfileTest,
   Boolean iisPermSetTest, Boolean iisPositiveTest,
   String iProfileName, String isPermSetName,
   String iExceptionTypeName, String iExceptionMessage, String
   iFriendlyMessage iAssertEqualsValue) {
         this.isProfileTest = iisPositiveTest;
         this.isPermSetTest = iisPermSetTest;
         this.isPositiveTest = iisPositiveTest;
         this.profileName = iProfileName;
         this.permSetName = isPermSetName;
         this.exceptionTypeName = iExceptionTypeName;
         this.exceptionMessage = iExceptionMessage;
         this.friendlyMessage = iFriendlyMessage;
         this.assertEqualsValue = iAssertEqualsValue;
      }
   }

   private List<PermissionTestData> PTD = new
List<PermissionTestData>();

   private List<PermissionTestData> setPopulatedTestData() {
      PTD.add(new PermissionTestData(true, false, true,
         'support', '', '', '',
         'Expected this test to pass'));
      PTD.add(new PermissionTestData(true, true, true, 'support',
         'Support Manager', 'ExampleCodeException',
         'No access for you',
         'Did not expect this test to pass as the permission set
involved should not pass!'));
   }

   @isTest static void test_getBankAccount_WithPermSets() {
      for(PermissionTestData p: setPopulatedTestData()) {
```

```
exampleCode instance = new ExampleCode();
User u;
Boolean didCatchException;
Integer result;
Account a = (Account)TestFactory.createSObject(new Account());
if(p.isPermSetTest && p.isProfileTest
    && p.profileName != '' && p.permSetName != ''){
    u = UserTestFactory.getUserWithProfileAndPermSets
(p.profileName, new List<String>{p.permSetName});
} else if (p.isProfileTest && p.profileName != ''){
    u = UserTestFactory.getUserWithProfile(p.profileName);
}
Test.startTest();
System.runAs(u){
    if(p.isPositiveTest) {
        result = instance.getBankAccount(a);
    } else {
        try {
            result = instance.getBankAccount(a);
        } catch(Exception e) {
            if(e.getTypeName() == p.exceptionTypeName &&
                e.getMessage().containsIgnoreCase(p.exceptionMessage)){
                didCatchException = true;
            }
        }
    }
}
Test.stopTest();

if(p.isPositiveTest){
    System.AssertEquals(p.AssertEquals, Result,
p.friendlyMessage);
} else {
    System.assert(didCatchException, p.friendlyMessage);
}
    }
}
```

A test setup like this has some upfront costs, namely writing the inner class
data structure and thinking through what commonalities exist across your
permissions-based tests. In the end though, it's much easier to maintain such a suite
of tests, as you can add or modify the .add calls in setPermissionTestData much
faster than writing a net-new test.

Assertions

If you take nothing else away from this chapter, let it be this — tests without assertions are not tests, but liabilities. Without the assert calls, you cannot check the outcome of your executed code block to see if it functioned properly. That's why I refer to test methods without assert calls as liabilities. Inevitably, when the code fails for whatever reason, you're accountable for the consequences. At 3am. On a Saturday. It's even worse, if your code is mission critical and fails at the quarter's end! Practice safe testing, use asserts.

The Salesforce1 platform provides us with three basic assertion methods. The first method, `System.Assert(expression)`, evaluates the expression within for a Boolean `true` or `false`. Thus, you can use it like this:

```
System.assert(1 = 1)
System.assert(BooleanVariable)
System.assert(p != np)
```

The other two built-in assertion methods are really shorthand, convenience methods built on top of `System.assert`. They are `System.assertEquals(expected, actual)` and `System.assertNotEquals(expected, actual)`. These often read easier than a simple `System.assert()` call. Here are a few examples:

```
System.assertEquals(1,1)
System.assertNotEquals(false, BooleanVariable)
System.assertNotEquals(P, NP)
```

It's important to remember that each of these built-in assert methods can accept an optional final parameter that I call the friendly message. You should always use the friendly message option, as it will help you debug which assertions and which tests are failing. You will only ever see the friendly message when a test fails. To use the friendly message, simply add a string parameter to the method call; for instance:

```
System.assertNotEquals(P, NP, 'Oh noes! P = np means all cryptography
is flawed!')
```

Creating your own assertion methods

Often, it can be useful to create your own assertion methods. Complex comparisons of objects and situations where multiple assertions must all pass are excellent candidates for custom assertion methods. Creating an assertion method is as simple as creating any other method, but to be used as an assertion, the method must either return `true` or throw an exception. It's a good idea to maintain the friendly message concept, so it pays to accept a friendly message parameter. If your assertion method needs to throw an exception, use the friendly message as the exception's message. If, for instance, we want to build an assertion method that proves that two contacts are from the same household, we might write it like this:

```
@isTest
public class customAssertions {
  public class customAssertionException extends Exception {}

  public static Boolean ContactsAreFromSameHousehold(Contact
    firstContact, Contact secondContact, String friendlyMessage){
    System.assertEquals(firstContact.mailingAddress,
      secondContact.mailingAddress, 'MailingAddress: ' +
      friendlyMessage);
    System.assertEquals(firstContact.homePhone,
      secondContact.homePhone, 'homePhone: ' + friendlyMessage);
    System.assertEquals(firstContact.lovesCrankCalls,
      secondContact.lovesCrankCalls, 'lovesCrankCalls: ' +
      friendlyMessage);
    if(firstContact.fullName == secondContact.fullName){
      throw new customAssertionException('Full Names are
        identical: ' + friendlyMessage)
    }
    return true;
  }

}
```

Here, we're both compiling standard assertions that now must all pass as well as a custom comparison. If any of the three standard assertions called here fail, or if the custom full name comparison fails, an exception is raised and the assertion fails.

We talked about what asserts are and how to use them, so let's take a second to consider when to use them. All tests should have at least one assertion after the call to stopTest(). Better tests will have multiple assertions identifying, for instance, that the object returned not only had the proper record type, but that it was properly modified by the executed code. Best yet, are the test methods that include two assertion blocks in addition to the standard after stopTest() assertions, the best tests will include a block asserting that your test data was created properly. This is especially important as you try to identify falsely failing tests. If the code works when manually executed via anonymous Apex or the UI, but fails in the tests, you may have a problem with your test data. Asserting that X number of contacts were created helps you identify the problem.

Mocking

Mocking is the practice of substituting the standard implementation of classes and methods with stub methods that return a fixed value. Other development stacks have rich and robust mocking capabilities built in. Salesforce1, on the other hand, is slowly expanding into the mocking world. In fact, there's only one built-in mock interface for you to stub. Despite the lack of a robust mocking library built into the platform, the capabilities of the existing mock interface make unit testing HTTP callouts a breeze. Additionally, there are other, third-party, mocking libraries that work with the Salesforce1 platform. Libraries, such as FFLib_ApexMocks, found at https://github.com/financialforcedev/fflib-apex-mocks, allow you to stub custom objects and methods so long as you have written your class to implant an interface.

Let's take a deeper look at the HTTPCalloutMock interface. Like most interface implanting classes, there are required methods for you to implement. In the case of HTTPCalloutMock, we must implement the response() method. This method must accept a HTTPRequest object as it's parameter and must return a HTTPResponse object. How we stub that out is up to us. To use our mock object in a test, we simply call: test.setMock(MockObj). After that mock is set, the next callout made will automatically return our stubbed HTTPResponse object. Rather than cluttering up my org with dozens of classes implementing the HTTPCalloutMock interface, I like to code a factory class that constructs the mock for me:

```
@isTest
public with sharing class CalloutMockFactory implements
HttpCalloutMock {
    Protected Integer              code;
    Protected String               status;
    Protected String               bodyAsString;
    Protected Blob                 bodyAsBlob;
    Protected Map<String, String>  responseHeaders;
```

```
public CalloutMockFactory(Integer code, String status, String
  body, Map<String, String> responseHeaders) {
  this.code = code;
  this.status = status;
  this.bodyAsString = body;
  this.bodyAsBlob = null;
  this.responseHeaders = responseHeaders;
}

public HTTPResponse respond(HTTPRequest req) {
  HttpResponse res = new HttpResponse();
  res.setStatusCode(this.code);
  res.setStatus(this.status);
  res.setBody(this.bodyAsString);
  return res;
}
}
```

With this factory in place I can easily test callouts by using the factory to return a response as it's needed. For example:

```
Test.setMock(HttpCalloutMock.class, new CalloutMockFactory(400,
'Invalid Request',  ps_GuidResp_Tests.json_error, null));
```

Tips and tricks for efficient testing

Following the general pattern for creating your own test data outlined here: executing the tested code between startTest() and stopTest() calls and always including asserts in the tests will set you on a good path for useful, robust tests. This doesn't, however, mean that the tests are fast. To help keep tests fast and your test-code feedback loop tight, keep these tips and tricks in mind:

- If you don't need to, don't insert and query data to and from the database. Starting with winter '13, you can set a value for the Id field, so long as you don't try to insert it. This allows you to create an object, set its ID, and create other objects that reference it. The slowest part of any web-based application is historically the database, and Salesforce1 is no exception. If you can cut down your SOQL and DML, your tests will run faster.

- Use @testVisible. This annotation allows you to quickly and easily annotate private class variables and methods and then access their values or execute the code during tests. Here's an example of it in use:

```
public class exampleCode {
  // Private member variable
  @TestVisible
```

```
private static Boolean normallyHidden = true;

// Private method
@TestVisible
private static void cantSeeMe(Integer 3) {
  //do amazing things
}
}
```

- Find a general mocking library and use it. The more complex your org becomes, the longer it will take to run your tests. If you're mocking out objects and methods whose return values are crucial to the code being tested but not the tested code itself, you not only add stability to your tests, you know what the mock object or stubbed method will return each time! But, you also speed up your code by bypassing all of the code those objects would be running! Additionally, you should mock every single HTTP callout!

- Avoid using `@isTest(seeAllData=true)`. Here be dragons. This annotation allows your tests to view all of the data in your org. SOQL queries run in tests without the annotation cannot see your existing Accounts, Contacts, and so on. When you annotate `testMethod` with `@isTest(seeAllData=true)`, all bets are off. It's true that some areas of the platform still require `seeAllData=true` because those objects are not able to be created in Apex code. For example, you cannot create an approval process in Apex. To test your approval process or the code that submits a record for approval, you'll still have to use `@seeAllData=true`. This also reinforces the idea that you should be creating all of the needed test data in your test methods!

- Consider investing in a continuous integration system. Many **Continuous Integration** (**CI**) systems, such as Jenkins or `drone.io`, work well with the Salesforce1 platform. These systems run your tests for you, at periodic intervals or after specific events, like a Git commit. They help you keep pace with the other developers in your org and allow for integration sandboxes where your team's changes are merged together and the tests run. This helps you identify when another developer has made a change that breaks what you're working on before you try to deploy it!

- Always test your code with bulk data, but change the volume of data per environment. Proving that your code is bulk safe doesn't have to happen in production. Create a custom setting for `TestOptions` and create a numeric field titled `EnvironmentBulkSize`. Reference that custom setting in your test cases as you can see in the following code. Remember to set your sandbox's `EnvironmentBulkSize` option to `200` but set your production value to something like 5. The less the work, the faster the tests:

```
@isTest
private class ExampleCodeTests {
  TestOptions__c options;

  @testSetup static void setup() {
    options = TestOptions__c.getInstance('default');
  }

  @isTest static void someTest(){
    Account[] accounts =
    (Account[])TestFactory.createSObjectList(new Account(),
     options.EnvironmentBulkSize);
  }
}
```

Summary

Throughout this chapter, we covered in great detail the why, when, and how of writing unit tests. There's a lot of information and nuance in this chapter. However, I hope you can walk away with not only a grasp of the fundamental pattern for unit testing, but also its three subpatterns of positive, negative, and permissions-based testing. Remember as well that a test method without at least one assert method is a liability. Furthermore, it's likely not going to be useful in the long run. Use asserts liberally. Assert not only the expected response of the unit of code, but also the data you created. Once your tests are written and passing, you'll be able to deploy your code to production. We'll talk about deployment strategies in our next chapter.

6
Deploying Your Code

Writing code isn't quite half the battle; there's testing your code and finally, deployment, that is, moving your code from your sandbox or developer org to your production org. Over the years, Salesforce has added tools and methods to move your metadata, including code between orgs. We'll start with the oldest, most venerable tool and work through all three methods of deploying code to production. Throughout this tour of deployment options, we'll discuss the types of metadata that are not deployable via these methods. Specifically, we'll discuss the following tools for deploying your metadata:

- The Ant migration toolkit
- The Eclipse and MavensMate IDE deployment
- Change sets
- Packaging

What does it mean to deploy?

When we talk about deployment on the Salesforce1 platform, we actually are talking about the tools and methods for copying or moving metadata from one instance to another. Typically, this is from a sandbox or development org to production. However, technically, refreshing your sandbox from production deploys production metadata back into a sandbox. Under that umbrella definition of deployment, there are really about four methods of moving that metadata. Two of these methods are rather coder focused, while the other two are more UI focused. Unfortunately, each of the tools has its own pros and cons, and often it's impractical to unequivocally state which one is the best. Some of them are, by their nature, perfect for quick deployments of one or two files, but tedious and frustrating when moving 1,500 files. Others work well with continuous integration tools and yet others are the least effort for IDE users. With that said, let's start with the Ant migration toolkit.

The Ant migration toolkit

Anyone familiar with the Java ecosystem will immediately recognize Ant, the stalwart task automation and build tool. While other tools such as Gradle, Maven, and Ivy have recently eclipsed it in popularity, it is an incredibly powerful tool, not just for deploying Salesforce metadata, but also for automating continuous integration builds, packaging, and general workflow automation. Ant is both the name of the tool as well as the language used to define tasks. As crazy as it sounds, Ant is an XML-based programming language, and automated tasks are defined in an XML file. Traditionally, this is called `build.xml`. The migration toolkit from Salesforce is distributed as a `.jar` file and defines tasks such as `<sf:retrieve>` and `<sf:deploy>`. Salesforce tasks rely on two other files that you must also create. The `build.properties` file contains information like your username, password, and instance URL. The `package.xml` file contains the information related to the files and kind of metadata you want to retrieve or deploy from Salesforce. This `package.xml` file is the heart of the Ant migration toolkit, and it is where most of the work of deploying via Ant takes place. You might end up editing the `package.xml` file every time you deploy. Conversely, the `build.xml` and `build.properties` files, unless your password changes, are generally configured once per-project. Here is a diagram of the tools and files and their uses:

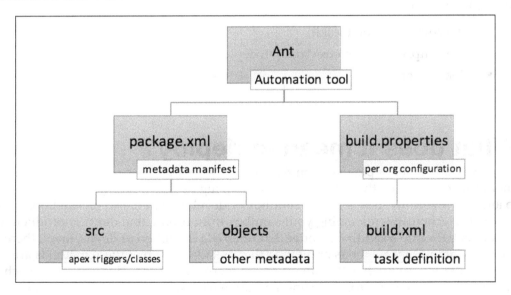

If all this seems daunting and complex, you're not alone. One of the Ant migration toolkit's biggest weaknesses is the sheer number of moving parts that all need to come together. Mix in handwritten, wall sized XML files and it can be very daunting indeed. Because the lion's share of work for an individual Ant deploy is in editing the `package.xml` file this method's greatest weakness is also its greatest strength. XML files are not only machine readable, they are also machine-writable. The built-in ability of most systems and development platforms to create XML makes this the best deployment option for continuous integration systems. Continuous integration systems can therefore dynamically create the `package.xml` files on the fly. A CI system can run all the unit tests in your sandbox and if they pass, build a `package.xml` specifying only the `git` files identifies as having changed. Deployment via Ant will always force all unit tests to run, but each deployment still has to parse and manipulate your uploaded metadata. Dynamic generation of package.xml files from git data is a nice enhancement, since fewer metadata components means a (admittedly slightly) faster deploy process.

Let's take a look at each of the three main files used in an Ant deployment. First, let's take a look at the `build.xml` file:

```
<?xml version="1.0" encoding="UTF-8"?>
<project xmlns:sf="antlib:com.salesforce"
name="Salesforce Deploy Build Script"
basedir=".">

  <property file="build.properties" />
  <property environment="env" />

  <!-- Include the ant salesforce migration toolkit -->
  <path id="classpath">
    <fileset dir="${build.dir}/build/lib" includes="*.jar" />
  </path>

  <!-- retrieve files from the source org and place them
in the build/src directory -->
  <target name="retrieve"
description="Clean the source directory and retrieve
metadata from source org"
depends="cleanSourceDirectory">
    <echo>Logging into ${sfsource.serverurl}</echo>
    <echo>With username: ${sfsource.username}</echo>
    <sf:retrieve username="${sfsource.username}"
        password="${sfsource.password}"
        serverurl="${sfsource.serverurl}"
```

```
                retrieveTarget="${source.dir}"
                unpackaged="${source.metadata}" />
    </target>




    <!-- Clean (remove all files) from the build/src directory -->
    <target name="cleanSourceDirectory"
description="Clean all metadata and directories in source directory">
        <echo>Cleaning directory: ${source.dir}</echo>
        <delete includeEmptyDirs="true">
          <fileset dir="${source.dir}"
includes="**/*"
excludes="destructiveChanges.xml" />
        </delete>
    </target>

    <!-- Retreives latest code into src direct and
 deploys the items from package.xml
 into the target org -->
    <target name="retrieveAndDeploy"
description="Clean, retrieve code from source org,
and deploy metadata to target org"
depends="retrieve,deploy" />

    <target name="deploy"
description="Deploy metadata from source dir
to target org">
        <echo>Deploying code from ${source.dir}</echo>
        <echo>Deploying code to ${sftarget.serverurl}</echo>
        <echo>Deploying code with username:${sftarget.username}</echo>
        <echo>Runing All Tests: ${sftarget.runAllTests}</echo>
        <echo>Deploy Root: ${source.dir}</echo>

        <sf:deploy username="${sftarget.username}"
            password="${sftarget.password}"
            serverurl="${sftarget.serverurl}"
            deployroot="${source.dir}"
            runAllTests="${sftarget.runAllTests}" />
    </target>
```

```xml
<macrodef name="git">
  <attribute name="dir" default="" />
  <attribute name="branch" default="master" />
  <sequential>
    <exec executable="git" dir="@{dir}">
      <arg value="pull" />
      <arg value="origin" />
      <arg value="@{branch}" />
    </exec>
  </sequential>
</macrodef>

<target name="checkoutFromGit">
  <echo>Issuing git pull from directory: ${git.dir}</echo>
  <echo>Pulling from branch: ${git.branch}</echo>
  <git dir="${git.dir}" branch="${git.branch}" />
</target>

<target name="checkoutFromGitAndDeploy"
  description="Checkout from Git and deploy to server"
  depends="checkoutFromGit,deploy" />
</project>
```

Let's break this down a bit and look at what's going on. This is a pretty boilerplate `build.xml` file for Salesforce deployment. First, we have a standard XML schema `definition` tag, followed by a `project` tag. Our `project` tag not only serves as our root node, but also specifies some project information like `name` and, crucially, the namespace. Ensure that your project namespace matches the one listed, or you'll have issues with Salesforce-specific tasks. Just inside our `project` node, we have tags for setting environment and build properties. We'll look at the `build.properties` files in a minute. Crucial to the success of your `build.xml` file is the `path` tag. Because Ant is a Java-based tool, you can extend your classpath with additional JAR files, and this path node does just that, loading all the `.jar` files in `build/lib/` and its subdirectories. Ensure that wherever you have saved the `.jar` file, which Salesforce distributes, is mentioned in the path node. I like to keep mine in `build/lib/`.

Targets, macros, and built-ins

Inside the `project` tag, we're defining a number of target nodes and one macro node. The target nodes define tasks that we can run with the Ant runtime. For instance, we can run `ant checkoutFromGit` to pull our code and metadata from a `git` repository. Similarly, this `build.xml` file defines: retrieve, `cleanSourceDirectory`, deploy, `retrieveAndDeploy`, and `checkoutFromGitAndDeploy`. Any of these can be specified on the Ant command line to fire off that task. Tasks can have dependencies, and if you look closely at the `retrieveAndDeploy` task, you'll see that it defines dependencies on retrieve and deploy. Dependencies are run in the order they're defined in and provide you with an easy way to combine several tasks into a more useful task. With our `retrieveAndDeploy` task, we specify the retrieve task and then the deploy task as dependencies. Nothing else is defined, however, meaning that when we run retrieve and deploy, we're actually running Ant retrieve followed by ant deploy. Astute readers will also notice nodes, such as `<echo>` and `<delete>`, which are ant built ins that help manipulate files and echo information back to the screen. Lastly, look at the `macrodef` node. Macros are Ant's way of allowing you to create your own custom shell commands as new tags. Our `macrodef` tag establishes an ordered list (`<sequential>`) of executable shell commands to be called. In this case, `git` with the three command-line flags specifying the `origin`, `branch`, and `git` command pull. You can just as easily specify pulling from a `Subversion`, `perforce`, or `Mercurial` repository. The `Macrodef` nodes like this one help make the ant migration toolkit best suited for automated, CI-type deployments.

Build properties

The `build.properties` file is a key-value flat file where you store information like your `username`, `password`, and Salesforce instance URL. Note that because this file contains your password, you should ensure that it's never committed to source control. Here's an example of a `build.properties` file:

```
# build.properties
build.dir=/Users/codefriar/src/AmazingPandas/

#sf target credentials
sftarget.username=codefriar@amazingPandas.example.com
sftarget.password=SuperS3kr3tP@ssw0rd+0k3n
sftarget.serverurl=https://login.salesforce.com
sftarget.runAllTests=false

#sf source credentials
sfsource.username= codefriar@amazingPandas.example.com.sandbox
sfsource.password=Like1'dPubl1$hThat
```

```
sfsource.serverurl=https://test.salesforce.com

#local properties
source.dir=${build.dir}/src
source.metadata=${build.dir}/package.xml

#Git branch to pull From (default is master)
git.branch=master
```

Conceptually, this file is much simpler! Each of these lines specifies a key (for instance, `build.dir`), and its corresponding value after the = sign. Note, however, that there are two sets of Salesforce credentials—a `target` set and a `source` set. The `target` set specifies the credentials used for deployments. The `source` set specifies where metadata and code are retrieved from. With a dual setup like this, you can easily update the metadata on your computer from the source org and then deploy to your production org. Note, however, that you're not limited to two properties. You can just as easily specify `sfIntegrationOrg`, `mySandboxOrg`, `StevesSandboxOrg`, and `JensSandboxOrg`. This would allow you or your CI system to pull and push metadata, code, and other information between all of the orgs your team is developing in, as well as the integration or testing org, and finally, production. You can set as many variables as you'd like here. Each will be included as `${variable. name}` within your `build.xml` file.

Choosing metadata

While the `build.xml` and `build.properties` files are relatively static, the `package. xml` file has the possibility of changing every time you make a deploy. At it's simplest, the `package.xml` file can be as bare bones as this:

```
<?xml version="1.0" encoding="UTF-8"?>
<Package xmlns="http://soap.sforce.com/2006/04/metadata">
  <types>
    <name>ApexClass</name>
    <members>*</members>
  </types>
  <types>
   <name>ApexPage</name>
    <members>*</members>
  </types>
  <version>31.0</version>
</Package>
```

This `package.xml` file specifies two metadata types: `ApexClass` and `ApexPage`. And,it directs the Ant migration tool to include all metadata of these two types in the deployment. Essentially, this `package.xml` affects all classes and pages. Note the package node's `xmlns` attribute. You'll need to specify this! The `Package.xml` files can specify any number of metadata types and is used for both retrieval and deployment. Thus, with a `package.xml` file like this one, when you make a retrieval call, you'd end up with a `src/` folder containing two subfolders—classes, which contains all of your Apex class code, and pages, containing your visualforce page source. Likewise, if you made a deployment call with this `package.xml` file, you'd be deploying the contents of the `src/classes` and `src/pages` folders.

The `Package.xml` files don't have to contain such blanket requests for all files of a given type. Indeed, your `package.xml` can specify specific objects and metadata files. For instance consider the following example:

```xml
<?xml version="1.0" encoding="UTF-8"?>
<Package xmlns="http://soap.sforce.com/2006/04/metadata">
  <types>
    <members>MyPageController</members>
    <members>TestFactory</members>
    <name>ApexClass</name>
  </types>
  <types>
    <members>Test_Page</members>
    <name>ApexPage</name>
  </types>
  <types>
    <members>AmazingObject__c</members>
    <members>Account</members>
    <name>CustomObject</name>
  </types>
  <version>31.0</version>
</Package>
```

This `package.xml` file specifies specific files and custom objects to retrieve or deploy. Additionally, it specifies the API version these should be retrieved or deployed with. This highlights an additional feature of the Ant toolkit. It's able to retrieve and deploy not just code, but almost the entire metadata of your org including custom objects, triggers, classes, page layouts, and at specific, API versions. Sadly, the Ant migration tool does have its limitations. Chief among them is its reliance on the Salesforce metadata API. This API has a number of incompatible metadata types that are listed here: `https://developer.salesforce.com/docs/atlas.en-us.api_meta.meta/api_meta/meta_unsupported_types.htm`.

Alas, I have become destructiveChanges.xml, destroyer of orgs

The Ant migration toolkit has one other crucial feature that is especially well suited for automated processes, and one that is unique to Ant and Force.com deployments: Destructive changes. Destructive changes require their own XML file. Syntactically identical to a `package.xml` file, it defines the metadata components to be deleted from the system. When deleting metadata, it can be important to define the order of destructive changes in relationship to additions. Because of this, destructive changes can be defined in any of three filenames: `destructiveChanges.xml`, `destructiveChangesPre.xml`, or `destructiveChangesPost.xml`. The `pre` and `post` options allow you to specify destructive changes to be made before or after the addition of new or updated metadata. If you do not specify `pre` or `post` in the filename, *the system defaults to doing destructive changes before additions and updates.* If you want to only do a destructive change, your `package.xml`, must contain no metadata components but must specify an API version.

Despite the verbosity of XML and unsupported metadata types, the ant migration toolkit is the most versatile and tested of the deployment solutions available to us. Additionally, because of the machine-readable and writable nature of XML, the ant migration toolkit is the de facto standard for doing deployments from an automated continuous integration system. The Ant toolkit and its various configuration files are an essential tool for Salesforce1 developers, and those that truly master it unlock the ability to not only deploy code, but remove it as well. This helps orgs maintain a clear understanding of what code is active — inactive code should be removed!

The Force.com IDE deployments

Several years ago, Salesforce released an Eclipse IDE plugin that, among other things, enabled developers to retrieve, deploy, and test code from within the IDE. This was later prepackaged with Eclipse as the Force.com IDE. Under the covers, the plugin exercises the same metadata API that the ant migration toolkit uses. The key differences between the IDE plugin and using the ant migration toolkit boil down this — the IDE takes care of creating the `package.xml` file from choices you make in the IDE's graphical user interface. The steps for deploying from within the IDE may not be intuitive at first. First, you select the metadata files you wish to deploy in the package explorer panel to the left. Once selected, click on the **deploy** button on the toolbar and walk through the wizard window that appears, as shown in the following screenshot:

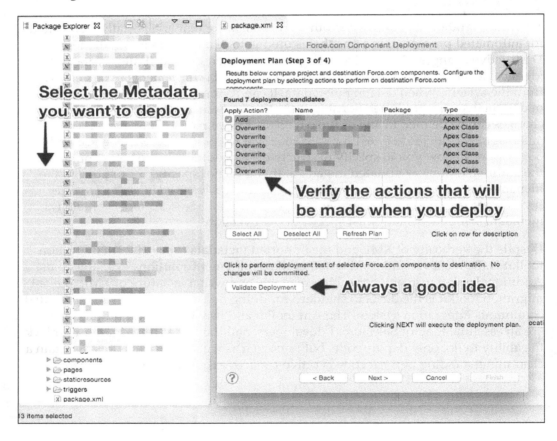

The wizard will prompt you to provide credentials for the target org and then ask you if you'd like to create a backup before deploying. Once you've answered those questions, it will log in to the target org and compare the metadata to present you with the preceding window. Here, you'll need to check each of the individual boxes to include them in the deployment. Also, ensure that the action specified makes sense for your org. If you think you're adding a class, but the action lists it as an update, it's likely a coworker beaten you to the punch. When you're satisfied that you understand the changes that are about to happen, click on **next** to start the deployment.

If you're intimidated by editing complex XML files, the Force.com IDE offers a friendlier, guided deploy system that is capable of both additive and destructive changes. This comes with a price, however, as the Force.com IDE plugin requires you to use older versions of Eclipse. On the other hand, if you're familiar with Eclipse, this may be the perfect tool for you.

In the last few years, other IDEs or IDE plugins have been created. First among them is the open source MavensMate for Sublime Text and Atom. Like the Force.com IDE, MavensMate utilizes the metadata API to do deployments. Unfortunately, MavensMate doesn't currently expose a graphical interface for doing destructive changes. The following screenshot shows the deploy options to validate the deployment:

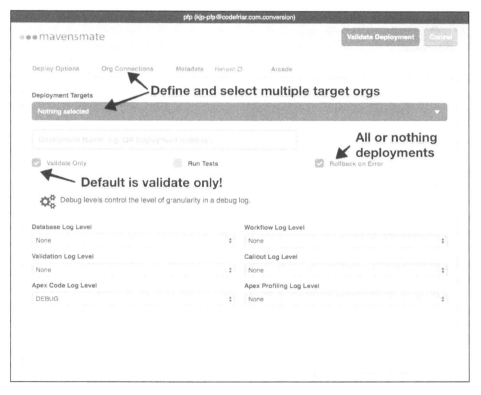

The process of deploying is a bit different with MavensMate. Rather than preselecting the metadata that you want to deploy, you're first presented with a rich set of options for your deployment. By default, deploys are set to **Validate only**, and **Rollback on Error**. Validation is always a great idea before finally deploying and using rollback on error, meaning that you won't end up with a half completed deploy. MavensMate uses tabs to separate parts of the deployment process. You can use the second tag to establish and edit org connections that are then selected (including multiple targets at a time) on the first tab at the top. Once you've specified the target orgs, use the metadata tab to select the metadata components that you want to deploy. Take a look at the following screenshot as an example:

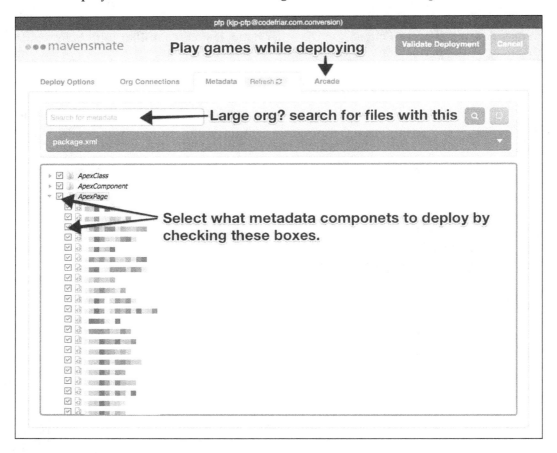

I've selected all of the **ApexPage**, **ApexClass**, and **ApexComponent** metadata types. However, if I wanted, I could deselect individual files within those types. After arduously setting up the deployment, you can relax on the **Arcade** tab with some classic 8-bit arcade games. Don't worry, as soon as the deployment is validated or completed, you'll be taken to the results.

Change is good

While deployments based on Ant and IDE are the backbone and time-tested processes for deploying Salesforce metadata, Salesforce has added a new cloud-based deployment solution known as Change Sets. Change Sets, as their name implies, are bundles of metadata created or updated in a source org that are made available inside another org. At its core, Change Sets work by establishing trust relationships between orgs and passing changes between them. These are referred to as **Deployment Connections** and can be found at **deploy | deployment settings | Setup**.

Note the **Upload Authorization Direction** section. The green arrow indicates that a relationship exists and is authorized, in this case, to move metadata from the **Conversion** sandbox to production. Editing a particular record allows you to establish relationships and set their direction. Keep in mind, however, that Change Sets can only be passed between related orgs, and only those sandboxes created from a production instance are eligible to be related. This means you cannot utilize Change Sets to deploy metadata from one production org to another.

Change Sets can work in both directions, for example, from **Sandbox** to **Production** as well as **Production** to **Sandboxes**. This makes them ideal for passing declarative metadata such as page layouts, custom fields, and objects from production orgs to sandboxes without refreshing the entire sandbox. To keep busy coworkers from accidently overwriting metadata, Change Sets have both outbound and inbound formulations. Outbound Change Sets are Change Sets of metadata from this org, destined for a different org. Conversely, inbound Change Sets contain metadata from a different org for potential inclusion in the current org. I say *potential*, because Change Sets are a two-part deployment process. You must first create an outbound Change Set, then log into the target org, and validate and deploy the inbound Change Set in the destination org. Creating a Change Set can be tedious and there are a few things to keep in mind. Once a Change Set has been uploaded, it cannot be modified. You can, however, clone it and modify its contents. Because of this, it's useful to include a version number in your change set's name. Take the following screenshot as an example for editing the Change Set:

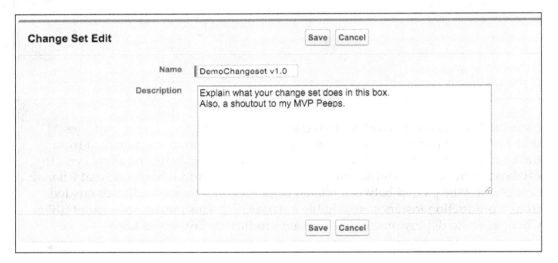

As you can see here, I've included `v1.0` in the **Name** field of the Change Set so that I can keep track of which one I'm validating in the target org.

Adding components to a Change Set can get tedious, but it's pretty simple. The UI presents you with a drop-down menu of component types. Once selected, you'll see a list view of metadata matching that component type, as shown here:

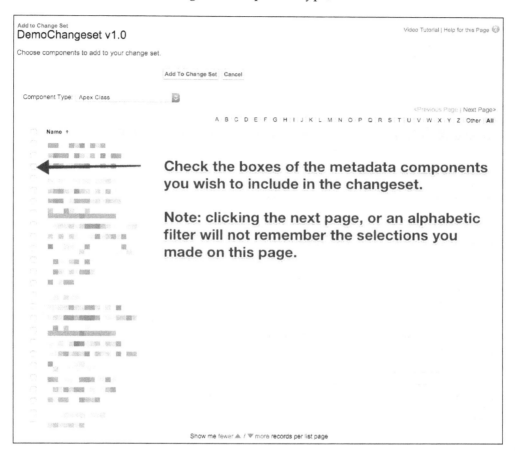

Check the boxes of the metadata components you wish to include in the changeset.

Note: clicking the next page, or an alphabetic filter will not remember the selections you made on this page.

Once you've added all your metadata components, you can upload the Change Set to any org you've established a relationship with. Once uploaded, it can take a few minutes for your outbound Change Set to migrate to an inbound Change Set in the target org. Helpfully, you'll get an e-mail message letting you know when the Change Set is available in the target org. Note that while you can create a Change Set with only metadata components, you almost always want to deploy the changes along with the profiles that will be affected by those changes. As tedious as creating large Change Sets can be, it's nothing compared to manually editing the field level security for the 30 new fields you just deployed for 5 profiles. Just under the component listing is the listing of profiles that will be deployed in the Change Set. Ensure that you always populate it.

Once your Change Set is available in the target org, you must validate and deploy it. Validation consists of mock deploying the new or updated metadata components and running all of your unit tests. While it's possible to trigger a direct deployment of a Change Set, validating your Change Set before deploying has its benefits. Not only are you prepared for any errors before they potentially affect your production org, it allows for nearly instantaneous deployments that bypass running all *tests if you've previously validated the change set in the last 24 hours*. If your orgs tests take hours to run, validation of a change set allows you to validate overnight, and deploy after a glorious cup of coffee in the morning. The following screenshot gives the status of the deployment:

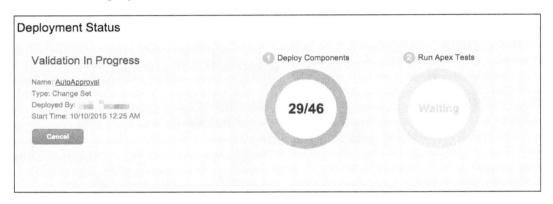

Overall, Change Sets are a fantastic tool for the bidirectional deployment of metadata from one org to another. This is especially true for highly regulated environments as Change Sets maintain a log of who deployed what, when. However, they are not without their limitations. First and foremost is the inability to make destructive changes via a Change Set. You can add new metadata and deploy updated metadata via Change Sets, but whatever is currently there cannot be removed with a Change Set. Additionally, you need to ensure that your Change Set includes every last metadata component your code relies on. Deploying an object and some workflow rules? Don't forget to include the custom objects' individual fields. They're not automatically included when you select an object to deploy, and failing to include a field can cause the entire Change Set to fail. In a very real sense, Change Sets are very atomic, and consequently, they can be very frustrating to work with if you're used to IDEs and the Ant migration toolkit.

Summary

Regardless of the method used for deployment, the goal is to move your changes from your development sandbox to production. For smaller code changes, a single class and its tests, or for declarative metadata, such as page layouts and object additions, I prefer the public audit trail provided by change sets. On the other hand, if I'm deploying an entire features' worth of code and tests, I almost always go for an IDE or Ant deployment. And if there's more than one developer deploying metadata, I always automate the process with a continuous integration tool with Ant. Remember that the only way to remove metadata from a production org is through the Ant toolkit or the Force.com IDE. This is reason enough to learn the pointy details of the ant toolkit's XML files.

In the next chapter, we'll dive into using APIs to build integrations into and out of Salesforce. Integrations require extensive testing, but can ultimately provide your Salesforce org with quick, efficient, and powerful methods of manipulating data.

7
Using, Extending, and Creating API Integrations

Increasingly, development is less about individual programs and more about building and integrating entire systems of code. In this chapter, we'll look at using the Salesforce1 sObject API, the bulk sObject API, how we can extend the sObject API with custom endpoints, and you will learn how to call various APIs from within the Salesforce1 platform. Specifically, we'll discuss the following topics:

- The various methods for integrating different systems together
- Learning to call the Salesforce sObject API to create, read, update, and delete individual Salesforce records from outside Salesforce
- Learning to use the bulk API for integrating bulk data into our Salesforce instance
- Building our own custom REST endpoint in Apex, and calling that from outside Salesforce
- Building a REST client that we can use to quickly and simply consume external APIs from within Salesforce

In the beginning, we physically moved tapes around

When computers were the size of small houses and required their own nuclear power station to run, data was moved between systems on magnetic tapes. Because computing time was a precious resource, operations were often done in bulk. Over time, a common pattern emerged: extracting data from the database in bulk, transforming that data into a bulk, and finally, loading that transformed data back into the database in bulk. This process is also known as the **Extract, Transform, and Load** (ETL) process. The idea was to pull records from a data store, run some kind of calculation or transformation on them, and then load that data back to a data store. This worked not only intrasystem loading data from an internal data source, but also form intersystem, as extracted data from one system could be loaded from the magnetic tapes that were physically transported to the second system. In a sense, ETL was the first API. APIs are built from a combination of one or more data interchange formats and a transportation protocol. In the case of ETL, the data interchange format was almost always comma- or tab-delimited flat files. A delimiter, such as a comma, was used to separate record fields. Line returns were used to separate records. ETL's transportation protocol, was magnetic tapes physically moved between systems, buildings, and cities. Today, APIs are far more automated, utilizing transportation protocols that don't rely on people or machines moving data on tapes. Nevertheless, they fundamentally rely on the same two components: Machine-readable data and a transportation protocol. Modern APIs utilize machine-readable, text-based data interchange formats, such as XML and JSON, transported over modern transportation protocols, such as HTTP and HTTPS. In fact, these tools underpin not only APIs but the contemporary ETL tools built on them.

SOAP then REST – the evolution of modern APIs

In the early 2000s, two technologies—XML and the HTTP protocol—evolved together into a technology for remotely accessing data and procedures. Deceptively named **Simple Object Access Protocol (SOAP)**, it proved to be less than simple and far more procedural than the object-oriented. Still, for many years, it was the preeminent method of exposing and consuming APIs. Part of the allure of SOAP was the extensive tooling that surrounded it. API vendors distributed **Web Service Definition Language (WSDL)** files that tooling could generate object code from. Virtually, every language from PHP to Apex provided such WSDL parsers. This made it convenient, if not simple, to consume APIs. The Salesforce1 platform provides the `WSDL2Apex` tool, which has now been open sourced to do this conversion for you. While there are some limitations on obscure types of WSDLs, in general, if you need to consume a SOAP API, WSDL2 Apex will take care of it for you.

Newer APIs are almost always released by vendors as REST APIs. **Representational State Transfer (REST)** or RESTful APIs as they are sometimes called, are fundamentally very different from SOAP APIs. First and foremost, REST is less coupled, allowing for greater flexibility in things such as data interchange formats. SOAP, conversely is tightly coupled to XML and dictates that all SOAP APIs use XML for data exchange. In contrast, RESTful APIs can use a variety of data formats. JSON is the most common, but you can use Google's Protocol Buffers, Microsoft's oData, or even XML. Like SOAP APIs, RESTful APIs utilize the HTTP(S) protocol for data transmission; however, that's where the similarities end. While SOAP requests encode the action and data in the payload of the HTTP(s) request, REST uses the standard set of HTTP actions that map by convention to types of API methods. Most RESTful APIs follow the following convention:

HTTP Action	API Action
GET	This has multiple uses, but it is primarily used for data retrieval.
POST	This processes the incoming data; it is typically used to create a new record
PUT / PATCH	This updates a record
DELETE	This deletes data

 The PATCH action is a relatively new addition to the HTTP protocol. On servers or APIs that predate it, PUT is used.

In practice, these actions combined with formatted data allow you to **Create, Read, Update, and Delete (CRUD)** data. Because RESTful APIs are HTTP(S)based, their URL endpoints typically define the object as well as API version and (optionally) namespace.

I oAuth, therefore I am

Salesforce provides a number of RESTful APIs, notably the sObject API, but also APIs for bulk data manipulation and streaming updates. These APIs are uniformly secured by the oAuth 2 identification protocol. oAuth is a conceptually simple identification protocol, however, due to the nature of what it's doing, it's still relatively complex. oAuth uses a client key and a client secret in concert with the information you provide, such as a username and password combination, to establish two things. First, it establishes the identity of the app the oAuth server is communicating with is allowed, and second, the user who is authenticating. In return of proof-of-accepted-app and valid credentials, you'll receive an oAuth access token. This token is essentially a long, pseudo-random string of characters that functions as a proof of identity for a given app.

These tokens usually have a finite time to live, for instance, an hour, during which that token identifies you to the server for access. With RESTful APIs, you often have to provide this token in a request header called **Authorization**. Often, this value is predicated by an identifying string, such as oAuth or Bearer, Salesforce's RESTful APIs all utilize this mechanism for authorization of API calls. Specifically, Salesforce authorization headers should be formatted this way:

```
Authorization: Bearer XXXXXXXXXXXXXXXXXXXXXXXXXXXXXXXXXXXXXXXX
```

We'll be making use of this authorization header throughout this chapter, so it's important that we figure out how to authorize our API calls. In order to make dealing with REST calls easier, let's use Postman, a free REST client plugin for Chrome. You can get Postman at www.getpostman.com. Postman lets you define collections of REST calls and save them together. For instance, you might create a sandbox collection with an authentication call and an upsert call saved in the collection. Handily, Postman is cloud based, so you can access your collections and requests anywhere you've logged into Chrome. The foundation for any Salesforce collection is the access token request, so let's set that up now:

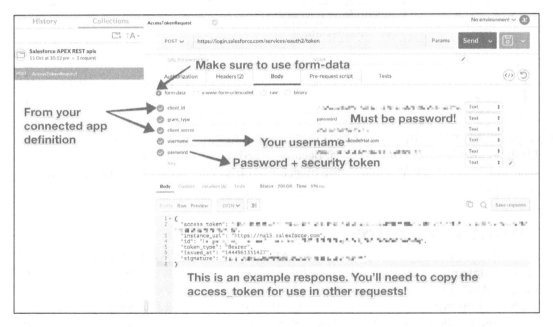

In the preceding image, you'll see the basic Postman interface. On the left-hand side is the list of collections and their requests. On the right-hand side, we have the interface for building a request. At the top is the HTTP action selector, in this case, set to **POST** along with the endpoint URL. For our authentication call, we'll need to **POST** our information to `https://login.salesforce.com/services/oauth2/token`. We'll need to pass certain parameters with the **POST** call and they are set up in the upper portion of the right-hand side pane. You'll need to fill out the following keys and their values:

Key	Value
client_id	This can be found on the detail page of your connected app
client_secret	Found on the detail page of your connected app
grant_type	Must say password this is not where you place your password
username	Your normal Salesforce username
password	Enter your password and security token here

Once you've filled in that information, it's time to hit the **Send** button at the top. If all goes well, when you scroll down, you'll see a JSON-encoded response containing your access token! It should look something like this:

```
{
   "access_token": "00Di0000000ap76!MYDAU6HT3R.T3S5A.
Isaw350m3AaBVlSd6sC30sYDoHS9_UTZK3_Mtj7TaIjtflXF96J3ybrrvVTqpU3rezCgjV
Fe56xdzY6m5AKht_d",
   "instance_url": "https://na15.salesforce.com",
   "id": "https://login.salesforce.com/id/NOTREAL0000ap76EAA/003i00000
00fm0Faq3",
   "token_type": "Bearer",
   "issued_at": "1444961351427",
   "signature": "8cTp+CtTAr3Y0uR3ad1ngThl$sIQHJg25gGSrivMKpYA="
}
```

This is the access token we'll need to authorize any other REST request we make.

Achievement unlocked – access token

Now that we have an access token, we can start to manipulate data. Because REST requests utilize HTTP(S) actions, and URLs to access data, we first need to understand how the URLs are structured. All Salesforce REST APIs share a common root, /services, and structure:

```
/services/API_to_use/version/object
```

Thus, /services/data/v20.0/query is a request to the query endpoint of version 20 of the data API. Likewise, a simple request for information based on a known ID results in a URI like /services/data/v33.0/sobjects/account/001i000000FOKzS and returns a JSON object containing the account's details. If you have a particular subset of fields or need to find more than one record, use the query endpoint. The query endpoint accepts a URL-encoded SOQL query and returns a JSON object with a results key. This array will contain the results of the query; however, only the fields you specify are returned. Importantly, however, each record will also have an attribute's object attached to it. This attribute's object details the sObject type and, most importantly, it's URL. Take a look at the following example of a JSON response from Salesforce containing the two fields:

```
{
    "totalSize": 1,
    "done": true,
    "records": [
      {
        "attributes": {
          "type": "Account",
          "url": "/services/data/v33.0/sobjects/
Account/001i000000FOKzOAAX"
        },
        "Name": "GenePoint",
        "Id": "001i000000FOKzOAAX"
      }
    ]
}
```

Here, in my SOQL statement, I requested Id, Name, as well as the attribute's child object, which I've highlighted. The url attribute is important, as it will become the url attribute we make update and undelete requests to.

Making the updates is simple. Make a PATCH request to the url attribute of the object you want to update. In your request body, send a JSON object with the fields you wish to update and the new values, as shown here:

```
{
    "name": "Most Awesome Company!",
    "industry": "Yak Shaving"
}
```

Likewise, deletion is equally simple. Send a DELETE request to the record's attribute url. It's important to note that these two requests return a response code of 204, no content, when successful. If you want the updated version of the record, you'll have to use a follow up GET request.

Creating a new record isn't difficult either, but it does highlight how the HTTP actions work. While we make the GET requests to retrieve data, the PATCH requests to update and DELETE calls to remove data, we use the POST action to create data. The POST request is really more like a process, in that it will process the request body in relation to the URL the request was made to. Thus, we can POST to /services/data/ v20.0/sobjects/Account/ with a JSON request body, as follows:

```
{
    "name": "Most Awesome Co!",
    "industry": "Alchemy: Turning Caffeine into Code"
}
```

In response, the API will give us an ID but not the actual record or its attribute information. Specifically, the returned JSON object looks like this:

```
{
  "id": "001i000001e1PyqAAE",
  "success": true,
  "errors": []
}
```

You can use the success and error keys to determine whether your object creation was successful or not. In the event of a failure, the errors key will be populated instructing you how to resolve the issue.

Putting it all together

We've talked about querying, creating, reading, updating, and deleting records via the REST API. There are a couple of additional tips that can make or break a REST API integration, namely, governor and location headers. Governor limits on API access can be confusing, as they're calculated on a rolling 24 hour basis. In response to this, Salesforce applies a header to every response titled *Sforce-limit-info*. This header has an easy-to-understand value that can be machine read:

```
api-usage=10/15000
```

This allows you to build an integration with the Salesforce sObject API and intelligently determine if you're nearing your rolling 24 hour limit. If you're nearing your limit, throttle back your calls. This prevents the potential loss of data as your integration loses access to the API due to governor limits.

Salesforce appends another custom header to data creation (POST) calls: the Location header. The value this header contains is the actionable URL for the object you just created. Rather than making an additional query request to get the new object and its modification or deletion URL, simply inspect the response headers for the location key.

One of the benefits of REST APIs is that virtually every programming environment has a robust HTTP(s) stack, capable of making requests to a URL and handling the marshalling and unmarshalling of data. This is so true that boilerplate templates have been created for common languages. Postman has these templates built in and can take your request and export the working code in a number of languages. For instance, here's a Java version (using OKhttp) of a create call:

```
OkHttpClient client = new OkHttpClient();

MediaType mediaType = MediaType.parse("application/JSON");
RequestBody body = RequestBody.create(mediaType, "{\r    \"name\":
\"Most Awesome Co!\",\r    \"industry\": \"Alchemy: Turning Caffeine
into Code\"\r}\r");
Request request = new Request.Builder()
.url("https://na15.salesforce.com/services/data/v33.0/sobjects/
Account/")
  .post(body)
  .addHeader("authorization", "Bearer 00Di0000000ap76!AQUAQDzVKaqKP4m
uP.AaBVlSd6sC30sYDoHS9_UTZK3_Mtj7TaIjtflXF96J3ybrrvVTqpU3KJPCgjVFe56x
dzY6m5AKht_d")
  .addHeader("content-type", "application/JSON")
  .addHeader("cache-control", "no-cache")
  .addHeader("postman-token", "e1ae9a9a-c842-42e4-4d10-
    8f470fb56531")
```

```
.build();

Response response = client.newCall(request).execute();
```

These created code snippets are great for prototyping mobile applications, but you should always ensure that you understand and approve of the code before putting it in a production environment.

Bulk data for everyone! Look under your seat!

Sooner or later, you'll surely to have to do a data load. The dataloader tools available for Salesforce are both legion and, for the most part, fantastic; in a way they're the last vestiges of the L in ETL. Unfortunately, while most dataloaders are to some extent scriptable and schedulable, they are not truly APIs. They generally require generating a CSV file as an intermediary step. Newer dataloader systems use the bulk data API, but they have historically utilized the standard sObject REST or SOAP APIs. In contrast to the oAuth authenticated RESTful sObject API, the bulk data API is designed to authenticate via a SOAP call. Additionally, it is architected in a way that facilitates data loads from external systems and applications in a much faster and more efficient manner than the standard sObject API. This efficiency comes from the ability to process multiple batches of data in parallel. Let's compare the standard sObject REST API and the bulk data API side by side:

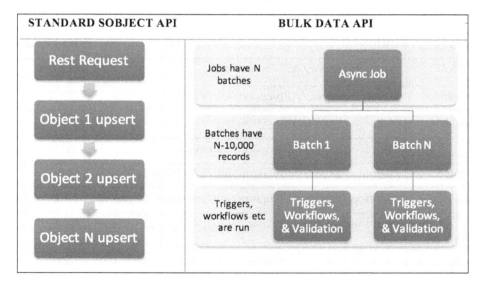

Uploading using the standard sObject rest API is done sequentially. Summer '15 introduced the ability to do this in a single call using the `/composite/batch` resource, but even with this, the records are still processed sequentially. In other words, each object's upsert has its own potential cascade of triggers, workflow rules, and so on, that must complete before the next record is processed. This is fine for 5-10 records, but it fails with hundreds or thousands of records. In contrast, the bulk API requires multiple requests, first to create a job and then to upload batches of data. These batches, however, can contain up to 10,000 records each. Additionally, you can submit up to 5,000 batches in a rolling 24-hour period. In effect, allowing you to upload 50 million records a day! What's even more amazing is that these batches are processed in parallel with each other.

To use the bulk API, you'll first need to authenticate. Like the sObject API, once we've authenticated, we'll pass our credentials via a request header. Unlike the sObject API, the bulk API does not use the authentication header, but rather a custom header titled X-SFDC-Session. To get your session ID, utilize the SOAP API's login method, which returns the session ID.

One you've authenticated, you can create a job. Jobs act as the parent record for batches, and give you insight into the overall progress of the data load. Once you've created a job, you'll need to add batches to it. Batches are essentially just data with a reference to their parent job. However, like jobs, it's possible to use the batch ID and the bulk API to monitor an individual batch. Create and monitor these objects using the following resource URIs and HTTP actions:

Purpose	URI	HTTP Action
Create Job	/services/async/APIversion/job	POST
Close Job	/services/async/APIversion/job/jobId	POST
Job Details	/services/async/APIversion/job/jobId	GET
Abort	/services/async/APIversion/job/jobId	POST
Add Batch	/services/async/APIversion/job/jobid/batch	POST
Batch Details	/services/async/APIversion/job/jobid/batch/batchId	GET
Details for all batches	/services/async/APIversion/job/jobid/batch	GET
Batch Results	/services/async/APIversion/job/jobid/batch/batchId/result	GET

If you look carefully at those URI and action pairs, you'll notice that a couple of them seem to be identical. This isn't a mistake. Remember that **POST**, should be understood as 'process this data'. Post calls always require data to be sent and the content of that data is what differentiates a close job request and an abort request. I want to draw your attention to these post requests, as that's where your input matters the most.

To create a job, the request body must contain a well-formatted XML document describing a `JobInfo` object, with three information nodes, `operation`, `object`, and `contentType`. An operation can be any *one* of the following: `insert`, `upsert`, `update`, and `delete`. It's important to keep your operation value lowercase, as `Insert` or `Update` will fail. The object specifies which of your org's objects, standard or custom, to manipulate. This field is *not* case sensitive. Finally, you'll need to explicitly specify the data's `contentType`. Your options here are XML, CSV, ZIP_XML, and ZIP_CSV. The ZIP versions are for objects with binary attachments! Here's an example POST request body to create a new CSV-based bulk upsert job on `Contact`:

```
<?xml version="1.0" encoding="UTF-8"?>
<jobInfo
    xmlns="http://www.force.com/2009/06/asyncapi/dataload">
 <operation>upsert</operation>
 <object>Contact</object>
 <contentType>CSV</contentType>
</jobInfo>
```

POSTing this request body to `/services/async/35.0/job` would result in a response similar to this:

```
<?xml version="1.0" encoding="UTF-8"?>
<jobInfo
    xmlns="http://www.force.com/2009/06/asyncapi/dataload">
 <id>750D00000000023IAF</id>
 <operation>upsert</operation>
 <object>Contact</object>
 <state>Open</state>
 <contentType>CSV</contentType>
</jobInfo>
```

Two fields are especially important in this response: the `id` and the `state` fields. We need the ID to add batches to this job, and the state tells us whether or not the job is open for new batches. Closing a job prevents other batches from being added. Armed with our job's ID, we can now start adding batches with POST requests to:

```
/services/async/35.0/job/750D00000000023IAF/batch
```

Because our job is set to use CSV data, our POST request body looks like this:

```
FirstName,LastName,Title,ReportsTo.Email,Birthdate,Description
Stephanie,Poorman,Senior Director Poorman family, herself@example.
com,1984-06-07Z,"Best darn wife this side of pluto"
Tessa,Poorman,Destructosaurus,parents@poormans.com,2014-03-11,"World-
renowned expert in toddling about and making messes."
```

In response to that request, you'll receive an XML response with details of the batch, like this:

```
<?xml version="1.0" encoding="UTF-8"?>
<batchInfo
    xmlns="http://www.force.com/2009/06/asyncapi/dataload">
 <id>751D0000000004fIAA</id>
 <jobId>750D00000000023IAF</jobId>
 <state>Queued</state>
 <createdDate>2015-10-14T18:15:59.000Z</createdDate>
 <systemModstamp>2015-10-14T18:15:59.000Z</systemModstamp>
 <numberRecordsProcessed>0</numberRecordsProcessed>
</batchInfo>
```

With the id atrribute returned by the batch creation post, we can grab its details with a GET request to:

```
/services/async/35.0/job/750D00000000023IAF/batch/751D0000000004fIAA
```

Such a get request will return largely the same information the creation call gave, but with up-to-the-minute data. Once the batch progresses from the queued status through in process all the way to finished, we can query for results. Now that we have at least one batch associated with our job, we can close or abort it. Closing the job requires a payload like this:

```
<?xml version="1.0" encoding="UTF-8"?>
<jobInfo xmlns="http://www.force.com/2009/06/asyncapi/dataload">
 <state>Closed</state>
</jobInfo>
```

Having closed the job, we've covered the life cycle of the bulk API—creating a job, adding batches, and closing the job. Monitoring jobs and their batches can be done in the UI by visiting the bulk data load jobs page in setup.

All good things have their limits

It's important to know the limits of the bulk API before using it. Unlike the simple limits of the sObject API, the bulk API limits can be a little bit more complex. The first few limits are straightforward:

- You can only submit 5,000 batches every 24 hours.

- Each batch can have, at the most, 10,000 records.

- Importantly, the entire CSV or XML can contain no more than 10,000,000 characters. If your records contain a large number of fields, your limit won't be the number of records but the number of characters.

- Likewise, each field has a maximum character capacity of 32,000 characters, but the entire record must contain less than 400,000 characters.

- Dizzying numbers aside, the bulk data limits described at `https://developer.salesforce.com/docs/atlas.en-us.api_asynch.meta/api_asynch/asynch_api_concepts_limits.htm` also illustrate a neat trick. Note that batches can only be added to jobs that are less than 24 hours old. What's not said is that once the job is created, you can add batches to it all day long, leaving it open until the day is done. This allows you to open one job per object and add batches as needed; this lowers your overall overhead call cost of using the bulk API.

Use cases for the bulk API

While the bulk API is vastly different than the sObject API, it still relies on RESTful principles; relying on endpoint URLs and HTTP action verbs to map actions. Determining when and where to use the bulk API isn't as clear as the HTTP verbs. In general, however, the use cases for the bulk API are different than those of the sObject API, so it's often easy to determine when to use it. Here are some guidelines for determining which of these two APIs to use.

It takes at least three API calls to use the bulk API: One for creating the job, one for adding the batch, and one to close the job. With those three calls, however, you can upload up to 10,000 records. Conversely, using the sObject API, you can only create 600 records in three API calls. Thus, the first guideline is based on the dataset size. If you have more than 600 records, use the bulk API.

The hardest cases to determine are those whose data source is transactional, for instance, an enterprise order system where the data volume of an individual transaction may be small, but the number of transactions may be high. In these situations, where the data source is creating two or three records at a time, hundreds or thousands of times a day, you have to evaluate the number of transactions against your available API calls. For instance, if you're creating less than 200 records, each transaction counts against one of your API calls. This is fine until you start hitting tens of thousands of transactions a day. If you start to hit one-third of your 24 hour API call limit, I suggest that you find a way to collect and batch these transactions into larger batches you can upload with the bulk API.

I always try to bias toward using the bulk API whenever I'm not creating a single record. My thought behind this is that if today I'm creating 25 records with this integration, when my company gets triple digit year over year growth percentages, it's likely that the 25 will be come 25,000 or more. Planning for the bulk API is admittedly a premature optimization, but at the cost of two API calls and a little bit of forethought; it's a premature optimization I'm comfortable with.

Creating your own API

Up to this point in this chapter, we've been using APIs provided by Salesforce. In effect, we're calling *into* Salesforce to retrieve or manipulate data. These APIs are well thought out, but they have their limitations. For instance, you can create, read, edit, and delete records, but you can only edit and delete individual records. Additionally, the tree creation endpoint, which allows you to create dependent, related objects in a single call, is only in pilot with the Winter '16 release. To help facilitate complex integrations, Salesforce has provided us with the ability to create our own RESTful endpoints, assigning HTTP actions to custom methods that accept custom payloads. We do this by writing custom Apex classes and annotating the class with @RestResource and individual methods with the @httpGet, @httpPatch, @httpPost, and @httpDelete annotations. To illustrate this, let's build a custom REST resource that accepts an opportunity ID and returns the opportunity as well as its opportunity line items and orders. Since this is a request for information, we'll use the GET action. Here's the general framework for what such a class would look like:

```
@RestResource(urlMapping='/OpportunityApi/*')
global with sharing class OpportunityApi {

}
```

Note the `@RestResource` annotation and its `urlMapping` attribute. This tells the system that we want this class to handle endpoints at `/services/apexrest/OpportunityApi/`. When our class is done and we want to use it, we'll make a GET request to that endpoint with an Opportunity ID specified, as follows:

```
/services/apexrest/OpportunityApi/006A0000009Yoed.
```

With that `@RestResource` annotation, our API class is now set up to handle routing at `/opportunityApi/*`, but there are no methods for it here. Since RESTful APIs use a combination of the URL and the HTTP actions, we need to add some actions to our class. Let's start with a GET request:

```
@RestResource(urlMapping='/OpportunityApi/*')
global with sharing class OpportunityApi {

  global class OppApiException extends Exception {}

  global class OppApiWrapper {
    global Opportunity opp {get; set;}
    global List<OpportunityLineItem> oppLineItems {get; set;}
    global List<Order> OppOrders {get; set;}

    public OppApiWrapper(Id oppId){
      List<sObject> oppFields = OpportunityApiFieldDefs__c.getAll().
values();
      List<sObject> oppLineItemFields = OpportunityLineItemApiFieldDef
s__c.getAll().values();
      List<sObject> oppOrderFields = OpportunityOrderApiFieldDefs__c.
getAll().values();
      this.opp = (Opportunity) OpportunityApi.
queryForRecords(OpportunityApi.generateSoqlFromCustomSetting(oppFiel
ds, 'Opportunity', oppId))[0];
      this.oppLineItems = (List<OpportunityLineItem>)queryForRecords(g
enerateSoqlFromCustomSetting(oppLineItemFields, 'OpportunityLineItem',
oppId));
      this.OppOrders = (List<Order>)queryForRecords(generateSoqlFromCu
stomSetting(oppOrderFields, 'Order', oppId));
    }

  }


  @HttpGet
global static OppApiWrapper GetOppOppLineItemsAndOrders() {
  Id oppId = OpportunityApi.getRequestUriId(RestContext.request);
  if(oppId.getSObjectType().getDescribe().getName().toLowerCase() !=
'opportunity'){
    throw new OppApiException('Provided ID was not a valid Opportunity
ID! passed OppId is: ' + oppId);
  }
```

```
      return new OppApiWrapper(oppId);
   }

  //Helper methods
   private static Id getRequestUriId(RestRequest req){
      Id UriId;
      try{
        UriId = (ID) req.requestURI.substring(req.requestURI.
lastIndexOf('/') + 1);
      } catch (Exception e){
        throw new OppApiException('Failed to parse ID in URI');
      }
      return UriId;
   }

   private static string generateSoqlFromCustomSetting(List<sObject>
fields, String objectName, Id matchId){
      String retValue = 'SELECT ';
      for(sObject f:fields){
        retValue += String.valueOf(f.get('Name')) + ', ';
      }
      retValue = retValue.removeEnd(', ');
      retValue += 'FROM ' + objectName;
      if(objectName.toLowerCase() == 'opportunity'){
        retValue += 'WHERE Id = \'' + matchId + '\'';
      } else {
        retValue += 'WHERE OpportunityId = \'' + matchId + '\'';
      }
      return retValue;
   }

   private static List<sObject> queryForRecords(String query){
      return database.query(query);
   }

}
```

I added a lot of code to our class this time, so let's go through it bit by bit. If you're going to code your own API methods, you should also include your own exception class, so I've added one. While it's certainly possible to build your APIs without wrapper classes, they come in quite handy here. Because Apex will automatically serialize the returned data to the serialization type specified in your request, a wrapper class becomes incredibly useful when dealing with API calls that return or receive multiple object types. In this case, the wrapper class does most of the work. This is done for a couple of reasons. First, to sanely encapsulate our API integration, and second, to keep our action methods pretty concise and clear. This has the added side effect of enabling further development, but we'll get to that in a minute. Most of this class is actually helper methods and our wrapper class.

Our wrapper class uses custom settings to enable admins to declaratively change the data that's returned by our API call. This is a trick I use wherever I can because enabling admins to change the number or configuration of fields returned by a custom API is a sure fire way to avoid countless please add this field e-mails. It's easy enough to generate a dynamic SOQL statement from the custom settings values, and you can see how to do it down in the helper methods.

Let's look at the `GetOppOppLineItemsAndOrders()` method. This method is annotated as `@HttpGET` and it's this annotation, in combination with the URI we request, that determines which method in this class is executed. Note that the GET and DELETE requests cannot accept parameters. You'll have to pull the `id` out of `RestContext`. This GET request `/services/apexrest/OpportunityApi/006A0000009Yoed` would result in the `GetOppOppLineItemsAndOrders()` method being executed with `006A0000009Yoed` as its sole parameter. Here is a diagrammatic representation of the previous example:

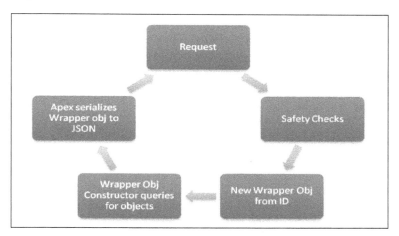

Let there be new records!

Remember I mentioned that using a wrapper class facilitates rapid development? Here's how it works. We've already established a constructor that generates an instance of our wrapper class and returns it to us. If we go one step further, we'll be able to accept JSON representations of our wrapper class for input! What's that step? It is a no operation constructor like this:

```
//no operation constructor for general deserialization from JSON
public OppApiWrapper(){}
```

With this no operation constructor in place, Apex will take our incoming JSON payload and attempt to deserialize it to an instance of our wrapper class. This means that our nested objects can be created with a method like this:

```
@HttpPost
  global static OppApiWrapper CreateTree(OppApiWrapper incoming) {
  if(incoming == null && incoming.opp != null) {
    throw new OppApiException('Incoming JSON paylaod failed to
      deserialize to an object with an Opportunity key');
  }
  //The point of this is to create object trees in a
  //transaction, so lets set a savepoint.
  SavePoint tx = Database.setSavepoint();

  //Try inserting just the opportunity. We'll need it's ID
  //to properly insert the child objects
  try{
    insert incoming.opp;
  } catch (DMLException dmle){
    //if we cannot insert the opp, abort the transaction
    //and throw exception.
    Database.rollback(tx);
    throw new OppApiException(dmle);
  }
  //Now that we have the opportunities ID we can assign it
  //to the child objects
  for(OpportunityLineItem oli: incoming.oppLineItems){
    oli.OpportunityId = incoming.opp.id;
  }
  for(Order o: incoming.oppOrders){
    o.OpportunityId = o.id;
  }
  //now lets try inserting our child objects.
  //we can do these together.
  //if either fails, abort the transaction and throw an exception.
  try{
    insert incoming.oppLineItems;
    insert incoming.OppOrders;
  } catch (DMLException dmle) {
    Database.rollback(tx);
    throw new OppApiException(dmle);
  }
  //Everything worked great! now lets return a new wrapper
  //object from our new opportunity
  return new OppApiWrapper(incoming.opp.id);
}
```

Letting Apex deserialize our incoming JSON into `Opportunity` and lists of `OpportunityLineItems` and `Quotes` allows us to focus on the mechanics and ordering the object's creation. Notice how this method is annotated with `@HttpPost`. This is the convention for RESTful API creation calls. If we end up throwing an exception, the response back to the client will contain our error message and be marked with an HTTP failure status.

Updating all that data

Convention holds that the `GET` requests return data, the `POST` requests create data, and the `DELETE` requests delete data. Updating data, however, is a bit more complex. In older HTTP servers, the only valid actions were `GET`, `POST`, `PUT`, and `Delete`. The `PUT` request became the de facto standard for updating data, if only because it was the only option left. Newer HTTP servers recognize the `PATCH` action verb for updating data. At the end of the day, however, the differences between `PUT` and `PATCH` are only name deep. The convention dictates that `PUT` and `PATCH` both function to update data; however, these days, `PUT` is increasingly rare in API documents. Thus, if we want to update data with our custom API, we should annotate it with `@HttpPatch`.

For an API to follow RESTful convention, actions that update or delete a record include the record's ID in the URI. In our case, this means that our update request endpoint is built from a `PATCH` action and a URI that specifies the ID like this:

```
/services/apexrest/OpportunityApi/006A0000009Yoed.
```

For Salesforce custom REST APIs, however, that's not required. The JSON payload you send with the `PATCH` request will usually contain the record ID. So long as your JSON payload keys match the input parameters of your method, Apex will automatically map them for you. Additionally, we can write the `@HttpPatch` method to accept our wrapper class, meaning our entire patch method looks like this:

```
@HttpPatch
global static OppApiWrapper remapChildren(OppApiWrapper incoming){
  try {
    upsert incoming.opp;
    upsert incoming.oppLineItems;
    upsert incoming.oppOrders;
  } catch(DMLException dmle){
    throw new OppApiException(dmle);
  }
  return new OppApiWrapper(incoming.opp.id);
}
```

This wrapper class is now doing a triple duty, allowing us to query, update, and create object trees. The only thing left to do is clean up after we're done with these records.

Another one bites the dust

Deleting data is, perhaps, too easy with custom rest APIs. It's a simple delete DML call. However, knowing what you have to delete and how you want to pass that data in is a bit more complex. In our case, we've created this RESTful API to function with, and on, an entire Object tree. Opportunities are the parent records for both orders and opportunity line items. As a result, the rest call we create only needs to delete the parent opportunity; the system will delete the dependent child objects for us. This isn't always the case, however, and if you needed to delete a tree of records associated through a lookup relationship, you'll need to identify those objects and delete them yourself.

Once you've determined what to delete, you'll need to set up your `@httpDelete` method to pull the record ID from the URI property of `RestContext` (or use a common helper method to do it for you). This is because the REST convention dictates that a `delete` request should be made to a specific record URI, and the Salesforce `@httpDelete` methods cannot accept parameters. Thus, we'll need to specify the record's ID in the URI as follows:

```
/services/apexrest/OpportunityApi/006A0000009Yoed
```

Thus, our `delete` method looks like this:

```
@HttpDelete
global static Boolean deleteObjectTree(){
  Boolean result = false;
  id UriID = OpportunityApi.getRequestUriId(RestContext.request);
    try{
        Opportunity toDelete = [SELECT id FROM Opportunity WHERE id =
:UriID];
        delete toDelete;
        result = true;
    } catch (DMLException dmle){
        throw new OppApiException(dmle);
    }
  return result;
}
```

This style of `delete` method adheres to conventions, but suffers from the same problems the standard sObject API has; you can only delete one record at a time. Throughout this chapter, I've talked about RESTful conventions, not REST rules. While the conventions are there for good reasons, sometimes you just need a bulk-delete method. In these situations, it's useful to remember that we can override these conventions and build our API method with a different action verb. Instead of calling `DELETE`, for instance, we can call `PUT`. Since you're the author of these API methods, you can ignore convention and code a `PUT` method that deletes the records specified in the JSON body. In fact, you can use `@HttpPut`, `@HttpPatch`, or `@HttpPost` to do this. Although you can, you should only overload the `PUT`, `PATCH`, and `POST` methods for destructive changes when you cannot otherwise help it. Let's take a look at what such a bulk-delete method might look like:

```
@HttpPut
  global static Boolean bulkDelete(List<String> ids){
  Id first = (id)ids[0];
  Schema.SObjectType sobjectType = first.getSObjectType();
  String sobjectName = sobjectType.getDescribe().getName();
  List<sObject> toDelete = Database.query('Select Id From ' +
sobjectName + ' Where Id IN :Ids');

  boolean SuccessfullyDeleted = false;
  try{
  delete toDelete;
  SuccessfullyDeleted = true;
} catch (DMLException dmle){
  throw new OppApiException(dmle);
}
  return SuccessfullyDeleted;
}
```

Here, our method is annotated `@HttpPut`, and we're sending JSON data containing which ID to delete. Our method has to pull sObjects from these IDs in order to delete them, so the majority of our method here isn't in actually deleting, but in finding the records to delete. Note the meta programming around the sObject name. Because we're pulling the sObject off of the first ID, we can technically use this method to delete any kind of object, but we need all the IDs to be of one object type. You can code around this, allowing for a bulk-multi-object delete, but I'll leave that exercise up to you. I want to stress that while this is an option, and one I've used successfully in the past, you should only break the convention if you absolutely have to.

The other way

So far in this chapter, we've used Salesforces' own APIs to manipulate data and we've constructed our own API methods allowing us to do complex operations specific to our org from the API. These are all fundamentally about requesting information from the Salesforce platform. This certainty opens up a world of integration options for us, but sometimes we need to work in the opposite direction. Where Salesforce becomes the client making requests rather than the API being requested. In order to do that, we'll need a good understanding of what it means to make http(s) calls from within Salesforce and how to handle the received responses.

As in the Salesforce world, so too external APIs tend to come in two formats: SOAP and REST. If you're making SOAP API requests, remember that the platform's WSDL to Apex converter will build not only your serialization and sending code, but reception and deserialization code all from your vendor provided API WSDL. However, if you're integrating with a REST API, we need to do some of the heavy lifting ourselves.

Heavy lifting

Making a callout from Apex involves three different objects: A `request` object, an `Http` object, and the `response` object. We'll need to make a `request` object, and in return, we'll get a `response` object from the `http` object when we send that request. When we create the request, we have to set the endpoint, the action, and any required headers. Additionally, we can send a JSON or XML payload body if required. Let's construct a simple `get` request to Google to demonstrate the mechanics:

```
public string getRequest(){
  HttpRequest req = new HttpRequest();
  //Set HTTPRequest Method
  req.setMethod('GET');
  req.setEndpoint('https://www.google.com?q=codefriar.com');
  //Create the http object
  Http http = new Http();

  try {
    //This executes the rest request
  HTTPResponse res = http.send(req);
  //Dump result to logs for debugging
  System.debug(res.toString());
    } catch(System.CalloutException e) {
  //If it fails, handle it responsibly
    }
}
```

This may seem cumbersome and verbose at first glance, but in reality, it's quite elegant, if very low level. To make this easier on ourselves, we need to create some intelligent abstractions on these calls. Ultimately, it'd be pretty handy to have `.post()`, `.get()`, `.patch()`, and `.delete()` methods at our disposal. I tend to refer to libraries like this as `RestClients`. Building such a `RestClient` would allow us to quickly and easily make REST requests regardless of the API we were integrating with. If we build it with object-oriented inheritance in mind, we'll have a library we can extend into specific classes for individual APIs. In the end, our call out REST architecture would look like this:

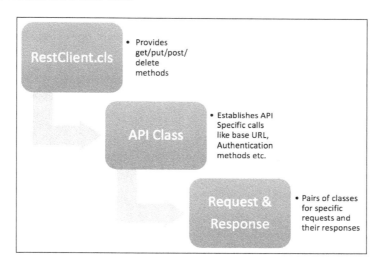

To build this, let's think through what properties, constructors, and methods a `RestClient` will need. Initially, we'll need properties for endpoint, body, method, and headers. These properties work together to provide all that is needed to make a REST request. We'll need a request generator method and execution and response handling methods. Since we'll want to be able to extend this, our class should also be a virtual class. Here's an example of what a basic `RestClient` would look like:

```
public with sharing virtual class RestClient {
  Public class RestClientException extends Exception {}

  Public Map<String, String> headers = new Map<String, String>();
  Public String endpoint = '';
  Public String method = '';
  Public String body = '';
  Public HttpRequest request;
  Public HttpResponse response;
  Public Integer responseCode;
  Public String responseBody;
  Public Http httpObj;
```

```
    Public String clientCert;

    Public Static Final Integer HTTP_MAX_REQUEST_TIME = 120000;
    Public Static Final Boolean ENABLE_DEBUG_LOGS = TRUE;
    /*
     * Helper Methods - These do the actual work.
     */

    Public void buildRequest() {
     if (ENABLE_DEBUG_LOGS) {
      system.debug('Restclient buildRequest details' + headers + '\n' +
        endpoint + '\n' + method + '\n' + body +
        'set RestClient.ENABLE_DEBUG_LOGS = false to suppress this
         message');
     }
     //Create the httpRequest Object
     HttpRequest request = new HttpRequest();
     //Set the max timeout
     request.setTimeout(HTTP_MAX_REQUEST_TIME);
     //Given a map<String,String> of header keys and values set
     //them as request headers
     if (this.headers != null) {
      for (String headerName : this.headers.keySet()) {
       request.setHeader(headerName, headers.get(hkey));
      }
     }
     //Set the Endpoint
     request.setEndpoint(this.endpoint);
     //Set the Method
     request.setMethod(this.method);
     //Optionally set the body, if it's not blank or empty
     if (String.isNotBlank(this.body) && String.isNotEmpty(this.body)) {
      request.setBody(this.body);
     }
     this.request = request;
    }

    Public void executeRequest() {
        if(this.request == null){
          this.buildRequest();
        }
        this.response = this.httpObj.send(request);
        if (response.getStatusCode() > 299) {
    throw new RestClientException('Response Code was: ' +
     response.getStatusCode());
        }
     }
    }
```

With this code, we've established some abstractions on the standard `http` callout functions provided by Salesforce. If we were to create a class extending our `RestClient`, we could make a request as simply as this:

```
public void makeApiCall(){
  this.endpoint = 'https://www.google.com?q=foo';
  this.method = 'GET';
  this.headers = new Map<String,String>();
  this.body = '';
  this.executeRequest();
}
```

This is easier to follow and less verbose, but it's not as fluid and clear as it could be. We can take and abstract this one level further, establishing constructors and methods facilitating development as fluid as `get()`, `patch()`, `put()`, `post()`, and `delete()`. Building out these methods becomes a fairly simple matter, for example:

```
public void get(){
   this.method = 'GET';
   this.executeRequest();
}
```

Of course, this assumes that you've already set the endpoint and other details. Sometimes this is a valid assumption, other times, we may want to have a suite of convenience methods in our rest class that allow us to set the relevant details and execute the request all in one call. Unfortunately, this means that many small methods must be added to our `RestClient`, like these:

```
public void get(String endpoint, String body,
  Map<String,String> headers){
  this.endpoint = endpoint;
  this.body = body;
  this.headers = headers;
  this.get();
}

  public void get(String endpoint, Map<String,String> headers){
    this.endpoint = endpoint;
    this.headers = headers;
    this.get();
  }

  public void get(String endpoint){
    this.endpoint = endpoint;
    this.get();
  }
```

Given these methods, any class that extends our `RestClient` has access to a set of `get()` methods accepting the full range of options. Thus, `get('http://www.google.com')`, `get('http://www.codefriar.com', mapOfHeaders)`, and `get('http://www.packtpub.com', 'body of request', mapOfHeaders)` would all result in a get request being made, and the instance's response object being populated. As an exercise for the reader, you can create similar method sets for `Put`, `Patch`, `Post`, and `Delete`. Additionally, you can write these messages to automatically encode sObjects into JSON request body strings.

I mentioned earlier that I like to extend my rest class with an API class, and that class with individual request classes. Once a solid `RestClient` is established, it can be used for any API. However, just about every API I've ever integrated with has had its own quirks, especially around authentication. Additionally, there are some intelligent abstractions to be made on a per-API basis. For instance, when integrating with the Salesforce sObject API, all of our endpoints start with the same URL, that is, `http://instance.salesforce.com/services/data/version/`. The API class can establish a base URL, instance, and version like this:

```
public virtual class sObjectApiRestClient extends RestClient {

    private final string APIVersion = 'v35.0';
    private final string instance = 'na7';
    private string baseURL = 'https://' +
instance +
'salesforce.com/services/data/' +
APIVersion + '/';
    private Map<String,String> additionalHeaders = new
Map<String,String>();

    Public override void executeRequest() {
       //first set our endpoint by prepending it with our baseURL
       this.endpoint = this.baseURL + this.endpoint;
       if(this.request == null){
          this.buildRequest();
       }
       //Having built the request, inject headers for authentication
       injectAdditionalHeaders();
       this.response = this.httpObj.send(request);
       if (response.getStatusCode() > 299) {
          throw new RestClientException('Response Code was: ' +
response.getStatusCode());
       }
    }
```

```
    private void injectAdditionalHeaders(){
      for(String h:additionalHeaders.keySet()){
      this.request.setHeader(h, additionalHeaders.get(h));
      }
    }
  }
```

By overriding the executeRequest method, we get to make changes to the way all calls for this API are made; in this case, setting authentication headers. This way, all calls made by this API class will be made with the authentication headers we need for this API. We can also insert the retry logic and the logic for authenticating if we don't have a valid oAuth token. This override does not change our get(), put(), patch(), post(), and delete() methods. Hence, individual call classes can still use the get() helpers defined in RestClient, even as their executeRequest method is overridden.

When the API-specific class has been defined, it allows us to create classes that make and handle specific calls. For instance, in the sObject API, we have an account endpoint. If we extend our sObjectAPIRestClient class with an sObjectAccountApi class, we have a single place to encapsulate and store all of our account-related REST API calls:

```
public with sharing class accountSObjectRestClient {

  sObjectApiRestClient restClient;
  private string endpointPath = 'account/';

  public accountSObjectRestClient() {
    restClient = new sObjectApiRestClient();
  }

  public string getAccountById(Id id){
    restClient.get(endpointWithId(id));
    return restClient.responseBody;
  }

  public string updateAccountById(Id id, Account account){
    restClient.endpoint = endpointWithId(id);
    restClient.body = JSON.serialize(account);
    restClient.patch();
    return restClient.responseBody;
  }

  //Helper methods
```

```
    private string endpointWithId(Id id){
      return this.endpointPath + id;
    }
  }
}
```

This is almost perfect! Our `AccountSobjectRestClient` class now has methods that abstract the implementation of how the API works. Once we've tested this, we'll easily be able to swap out the implementation of this API. There's one more thing we can do to make this usable—handling the translation of the response JSON into objects we can natively use. Writing JSON deserialization code is tedious at best and error prone at worst. Thankfully, a couple of amazing developers developed a web app that will automatically generate JSON deserialization code for you. Simply paste your JSON returned by the API into the box at `json2apex.herokuapp.com`, and name your deserialization class. When you click on **Create Apex**, you will download both the deserialization class and the tests for that class (yes, it generates the tests too!), as shown in the following screenshot:

Note the **Create explicit parse code** option. If your JSON requires explicit parsing because it contains, for instance, an Apex reserved word, this web app will automatically convert to using explicit parsing code. Because of this, you can effectively ignore that option. The code generated provides you with a static method called parse, which will return an object of the type you entered in the **Name for the generated class** field. In our example from the preceding screenshot, we'd receive back an object of the AccountRestResponses type. We can incorporate this into our accountSObjectRestClient class by modifying our methods to return the parsed object like this:

```
public accountRestResponses getAccountById(Id id){
  restClient.get(endpointWithId(id));
  accountRestResponse parsedObj;
  try{
    parsedObj = accoutRestResponses.parse(restClient.responseBody);
  } catch (JSONException jsone) {
    throw new RestClient.RestClientException(jsone);
  }
  return parsedObj;
}
```

Now, we have the full round trip package with a generic RestClient class with polymorphic versions for specific APIs that are used by object-specific classes with the ability to serialize and deserialize our data on the fly. With a system like this, you can integrate virtually any RESTFul API available. There are, of course, some limitations we need to be mindful of. The biggest limitation we need to track is the payload size. Asking an API to return 20,000 records may well be within the capabilities of that API, but Salesforce's ability to de-serialize and handle that many records depends on their size. Salesforce has a maximum response size of 6 MB. If your 20k records fit into a response of 6 MB, great! Otherwise, you'll have to request smaller batches of records. You also need to be mindful of the CPU time limit governor. If you can receive 20k records but not process them in time, you're still going to have to ask for smaller chunks. Regardless of its few limitations, the ability to make HTTP callouts to other APIs is an invaluable tool for building integrations between Salesforce and your external APIs.

Putting it all together

With a solid background in API principles and the ability to use the sObject, bulk, and custom API endpoints, it's possible to seamlessly integrate external data with Salesforce. While integrating into Salesforce is undoubtedly useful, it's only when coupled with calling out from Salesforce that the full power of API integrations becomes visible. The use cases are easy to imagine. For instance, a marketing mailing company may upload hundreds of thousands of contacts a day via the bulk API and process them using a batch job, which validates their mailing address via the US Postal Service's address validation API. E-commerce sites on the Salesforce1 platform can accept payment via various payment APIs and undertake order fulfillment via an integration with the company's ERP system. Google Chrome and Firefox extensions for Gmail can call in via the sObject API to let users attach e-mails from Gmail to cases, accounts, contacts, and even custom objects. You can even bridge media types using the API to drive call center phone dialers or send text messages. Any time you need to combine your Salesforce data with external data, APIs provide the easiest and often the best way to access it. Knowing which API to use and when to use it is the key to mastering their use. Let's take a look at the following diagrammatic representation of the Salesforce platform:

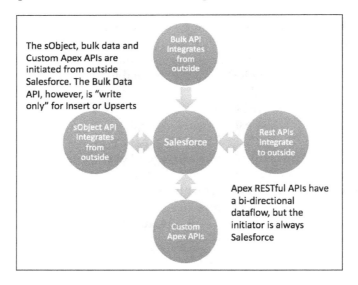

If the integration is controlled from outside Salesforce and is largely transactional, manipulating a single or at most a few dozen records at a time, the sObject API is the simplest approach. However, if your integration relies on massive amounts of data being inserted or updated, you'll need to use the bulk API. The general threshold is 600 records. More than that, and you should use the bulk API. Under 600 records and the choice between sObject API and the bulk API is yours. If your integration is controlled from outside Salesforce and manipulates complex sets of related objects or requires custom processing inside Salesforce, custom Apex APIs are your go-to option.

On the other hand, if the API requests originate inside Salesforce, making RESTful callouts to those APIs can be done using a generic `RestClient` class in conjunction with an API-specific extension and some individual request and response classes as we demonstrated. These callouts can be particularly useful in conjunction with batch jobs or other asynchronous processing techniques talked about in *Chapter 3, Asynchronous Apex for Fun and Profit*, to accomplish bulk data-cleanliness tasks. Additionally, they're fantastic for pulling supplemental information about contacts such as tweets, Facebook posts, or Instagram photos.

Integrations are perhaps the most crucial aspect to mastering Force.com development. The Salesforce1 platform has a staggeringly powerful declarative application development environment, and an equally powerful code-based environment, but it's the data that makes these features useful to businesses big and small. Getting data into and out of the platform for use is therefore the foundation for meaningful apps. The APIs we talked about in this chapter are just the start. The streaming, analytics, metadata, tooling, and audit trail history APIs all bring additional features and capabilities to the platform, but in the end, all APIs are centered around data. Building a robust set of portable tools such as a `RestClient` class, makes adding new APIs into the mix a much simpler and faster affair. Practice using these integrations and tools and you'll quickly find that you've learned not only how to manipulate data, but also how to do so at scale in the right fashion with the right tools. Additionally, as you integrate systems with APIs, you'll become quite the expert at asynchronous processing, bulk data manipulation, and a host of other Force.com tools and practices. APIs are therefore not only the tools for integrating different systems, but also for integrating your knowledge of the platform into a masterful architecture.

Summary

In this chapter, we discussed how to use Salesforce inbound APIs, such as the sObject and bulk data APIs as well as creating our own inbound APIs. We also discussed making outbound API calls from within Apex and how to structure our code to facilitate code reuse with a `RestClient` class as well as individual API and request classes. Together, these techniques enable you to programmatically pull or push data into your Salesforce org, allowing you to tie into other systems such as SAP, Oracle, or even the Postal Service.

In our next chapter, we'll dive into how we can work as a team on the Salesforce1 platform, including version control, continuous integration, and the process that ties it all together.

8
Team Development with the Salesforce1 Platform

It has become increasingly clear to me that collaboration will almost always trump individual genius. Working together not only makes each individual's workload lighter, but it also fosters cross-pollination of ideas and practices. This takes many forms, from classic teams with hierarchy and rank, to developers pairing with each other to collaboratively share a keyboard while writing and testing code. Regardless of the form you're used to, it is almost a certainty that you are not the sole developer for your company and that you work in some form of team. Over the years of software development, a number of issues have sprung up around team development and, as is always the case with software, more than one solution has claimed to forever solve these problems. The Salesforce1 platform is not exempt from this; indeed, some team development problems are exacerbated by the platform. In this chapter, we're going to take a small step back from the rigors of coding on the platform for a discussion of how to safely, effectively, and quickly develop on it. Specifically, we'll dive into:

- Traditional team development problems and their solutions
- A quick overview of version control with Git
- Modifying traditional solutions for the Salesforce1 platform
- Using continuous integration to automate source control and deployments
- Why naming, formatting, and common tool chains are essential

But we've always done it that way!

Back in the early seventies, an engineer at Bell labs released the Source Code Control System, or SCCS. SCCS was an early attempt at maintaining records of changes made to source code. SCCS gave way to Revision Control System, or RCS, and RCS in turn gave way to Concurrent Versions System, or CVS. Eventually, CVS faced competition from newer, distributed version control systems such as Git and Mercurial. Each of these platforms inherited one or more crucial ideas, or components, or from their predecessors while still bringing new features and innovations to the table. Regardless of their individual features and innovations, all of them attempt to solve one basic problem: tracking and maintaining the history of files and projects. These tools are collectively called **Version Control Systems** or just **Version Control**, but they lead to an interesting question: why track and maintain the history of text files? The answer is at once both obvious and non-intuitive. It's obvious that keeping detailed history helps you rollback performance degradations and bugs quickly and easily. Many also facilitate easy backup of your code to a networked server. However, I think the real win with detailed histories is the way they enable multiple developers to work on the same file. If you and I are both editing the same file, a detailed history can help us interleave our changes, incorporating without overwriting the changes each of us has made.

The differences between version control systems is largely found in their ability to handle changes across one or multiple files for each **commit** or historical record, and the way they handle remote repositories. For instance, SCCS and RCS are only capable of handling the changes of a single file at a time. CVS, on the other hand, is capable of **atomic** commits of multiple files at the same time. CVS also provides the ability to commit one's work to a CVS centralized server. Conversely, Git enables developers to decentralize their code repository, sending their commits to any number of remote servers or even other developers.

Maintaining a historical record of everyone's work is, in my experience, the single largest *problem* with team development. It's a problem because my work may be in the same file as your work. If I submit my changes while you're still making yours, there's a good chance that your changes will overwrite mine and my work will be lost. Likewise, my work may overwrite a change you made just seconds before I started. Rather than simply locking one another out of the file(s) we're editing, we need a way that fosters the ability for you and I to work on the same file, often even editing the same method at the same time. Version control is the historical answer to this problem, and today one of the most common version control systems is Git. We'll learn more about Git and how it solves this problem later in this chapter.

Having to maintain a historical record of a developer's work to ensure no changes are inadvertently lost is by no means the only problem facing teams of developers. There's an old joke about asking a group of five developers what their favorite editor is and getting back nine answers. We developers are *opinionated* on how and what to use to accomplish our work. Style is, to many of us, just as important as substance. As a team, the issue of code style matters because it affects how we view, read, and understand code, which in turn affects our ability to quickly and easily find, fix, and test bugs. Traditionally, these kinds of problems have been solved by style guides, or social contracts among developers to maintain a common style between files and projects. Some of the most popular languages have even published style guides. Ruby and Python are some of the best examples of this, especially Python's Python Enhancement Project 0008 or PEP8 guide. Social contracts are great, but they tend to suffer in times of emergency. Maintaining the social style norms can be a chore. Ultimately, we'd be better off with an automatically applied style.

Perhaps one of the most vexing problems teams face is the issue of naming things. The hardest problem in computer science, as the old adage says, is cache invalidation and naming things. I once worked with a brilliant developer; he taught me a good number of things, but his background was in assembly and Fortran on ancient memory-strapped systems. All his variable names were single characters: a, b, …z. Modifying his code was an exercise in whiteboard-symbol management. Another developer I worked with maintained strict Hungarian notation names, prefacing all variables with a single character identifying the type: iIntegerVar, boolean, and so on. His code was far easier to read and understand, but it still stood out against the rest of the team's code, especially considering the strict typing and tools the language provided. This posed a problem for our team as it routinely meant finding blocks of functionally-duplicate code. Team members didn't have a common naming scheme to look up objects and functions, so they duplicated functionality. The bigger the project, the more likely this kind of thing is going to happen.

Exacerbating the issues

Salesforce1 development is not immune to these issues of accidental code overwriting, inconsistent style, and problems surrounding naming things. Sometimes, in fact, the platform exacerbates these issues. Because the platform is cloud-based, the definitive copy of the code isn't stored on a central version control server, or even on individual developer's laptops. If developers are sharing a sandbox, even using the developer console won't prevent team members from overwriting each other's code changes. Other tools such as MavensMate, Eclipse, and the new Illuminated Cloud will prompt you before overwriting changes, but even this can't prevent the problem; it only warns against it.

While style and naming don't have the dramatic effects of overwriting code, they are nevertheless an issue that grows with the size of the team. Sadly, there's no platform style guide, official or unofficial. Likewise, there's no naming guide, and while Apex is case-insensitive, most file systems still sort capitalized filenames before uncapitalized filenames. This makes it hard to remember or find the class that you and your team want to extend or use.

Technology to the rescue – caveat audiens

Thankfully, each of these challenges have relatively simple automated solutions. Version control and the intelligent use of a continuous integration system will help us prevent code overwriting and provide a platform for us to automatically take action. From here on out, this chapter will be a bit more prescriptive than past chapters, exploring how to foster team development on the Salesforce1 platform based on my own past experience. Throughout this chapter, I'll identify some key principles that provide the foundation for this to work. Together, we'll overcome the many issues teams face, and the solutions discussed are, in my opinion, the best out of many.

The moving parts

Fundamentally, we have a single tool, and a single point in the development workflow to enforce style and naming conventions and to ensure no code is overwritten: **deployment**. However, if the whole team is sharing a single development org, we'll still have code-overwriting issues. The solution is easy, if unintuitive: every developer—even declarative developers—gets his or her own sandbox to work in. This is the first principle. If you're a small team in a small org, use developer environments rather than sandboxes. Regardless of the environment type, this entire model is predicated on every person who's making a change doing so in their own sandbox. Once the team is working in their own sandboxes, they can make changes as they see fit, knowing they'll never overwrite another developer's code. With multiple sandboxes, we now have multiple deployment points, or moments in which we move code from one or more sandboxes into one or more sandboxes.

Git is a contemporary version control system established by Linus Torvalds of Linux fame. It differs from other version control systems we've talked about in that it's a *distributed* version control system. Every person **clones** the repository to their local machine and begins working there. As commits are made, they are only applied to the local version of the repository. When the user is done with a number of commits, say a new feature, or some additional tests, he or she can **push** those commits to other copies of the repository.

Sometimes, those repositories live on internal corporate servers. Others live on public Git repository hosting company servers such as GitHub or BitBucket. It's crucial, however, to remember that remotes don't have to be dedicated servers; they can be the Raspberry Pi in your closet or your coworker's corporate laptop. Because of the dual commit and push system, developers are encouraged to routinely commit their work, even if they only push when features or fixes are complete.

Version control is our mechanism for ensuring that code isn't overwritten. However, in order to do this, we'll need a sane branching and merging strategy. This is the second principle: use a common and well-established version control branching and merging strategy. I've had great experiences with a Git extension named `git flow`, and it's common enough that most Git frontend tools that I've come across support it out of the box. Git flow relies on a central source of truth, a repository that all committers push to, called an origin. In our case, we'll use GitHub.com as our origin repository, but this works equally well with Bitbucket, GitLab, and like systems. Git flow expects that the HEAD of the master branch is always in a production-ready state. To keep it in such a deployable state, no modifications are made directly on the master branch. All work is done on a parallel branch named **develop**. New features are built off in named feature branches branched from the develop branch and, when they're completed, they're merged back into the develop branch. Hotfix branches, on the other hand, are forked from the master branch but crucially pushed back down, not only to master for deployment, but also to develop! As multiple features are completed, develop is merged down into master as complete deployable change sets known as releases. These relationships are evidenced in the following diagram:

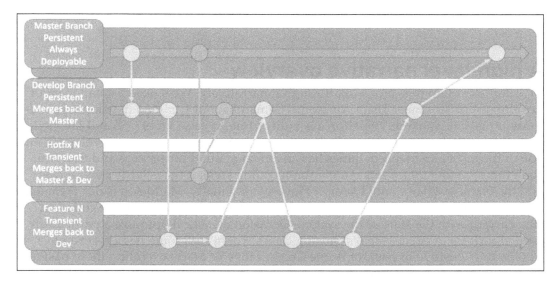

In this diagram, each dot represents a version control commit, including branch creation. There are three key takeaways from this branching and merging strategy. First of all, master is always in a deployable state and where we start our production deployments from. Second, we perform development on feature branches, isolating changes made for one feature from the changes made for another. Lastly, hotfix branches are branched from master but merged to both develop and master.

With our branching and merging strategy established, we can now talk about why this is beneficial. Git is a bit of a version control Swiss Army chainsaw. Like a Swiss Army knife, Git has plenty of options, features, and tools. Unlike a Swiss Army knife, Git can be awkward for new users and rather unforgiving at times, not unlike a Chainsaw. I like to periodically remind everyone that you can do anything you want or need with Git, including accidentally cut off your foot. The primary thing this branching and merging strategy gives us is predictability. We can harness this predictability during merging, which in turn allows us to largely automate things.

As I mentioned in *Chapter 5, Writing Efficient and Useful Unit Tests*, continuous integration systems work in conjunction with your version control system to automatically run your tests whenever you push changes. We'll use a CI system to not only run our tests, but trigger actions based on the results of those test runs. While Apex unit tests are first and foremost here, a good CI system allows us to run JavaScript tests and even browser-based tests. We can also harness the CI system to run what I call **meta-tests** for things such as code coverage in JavaScript, compliance with style, and naming conventions. Creating pull requests, enforcing style conventions, and deploying code from one environment to another will all occur automatically in response to test runs.

A high-level narrative overview

In order to explain this, let's walk through it narratively. We'll need a small team of developers, so let's meet Team Awesome. Samantha, our frontend developer spends most of her time making Visualforce beautiful. She writes a lot of CSS and JavaScript and most of that goes into Static Resources. James is one of our Apex developers, and one of the most experienced. James has an amazing mind for process and flow, but sometimes accidently forgets our common coding style. Jorge is fairly new to Apex and the team, but has a long history of Java work. Finally, Maddison is our team lead and architect. She doesn't often write code, but likes to keep up with the code and stay current with the state of the system. Occasionally, she'll optimize a particularly hard algorithm or process that's causing issues. Team Awesome has a record of tremendous positive impact for Acme Co., but they've been struggling these past few sprints with defects creeping up and code lost. To solve this, Maddison has decided to implement version control, continuous integration, and some new processes to help guide the team.

After explaining the Git branching and merging strategy and setting each of them up with their own sandbox, Maddison explains that the one full-copy sandbox Acme Co. has is now the integration and staging sandbox. As each of them make modifications in their own sandboxes, they're responsible for making sure their own sandbox passes all tests. When they commit completed features to their GitHub repo, the continuous integration system will ensure a suite of unit, style, JavaScript, and code coverage tests are run. If *all* the tests pass, a GitHub pull request will be generated. During code review, any of the team members can reject the pull request for any number of reasons. However, if they find everything acceptable, they'll accept it. Accepting the pull request triggers a number of actions. First, it deploys the develop branch, with it's newly merged feature to the integration and staging sandbox. Secondly, it generates pull requests from develop to all other open feature branches. Developers with open feature branches can accept the pull request to update and keep their working environment up-to-date. Accepting these pull requests not only merges the updates from develop into their feature branch, but it also deploys the updates to their sandbox.

Maddison is a bit concerned about the complexity of this system, so she goes over each step and makes sure everyone understands their roles and responsibilities. Each of the team members are responsible for four things. The first thing is only modifying code and metadata in their own sandbox. Two is ensuring that their code has valid, useful tests regardless of its language. Three is to actively participate in code reviews via pull requests. And finally, the fourth responsibility is to keep their own sandbox up-to-date by accepting pull requests from develop as they come in. Everything else, Maddison explains, is automated:

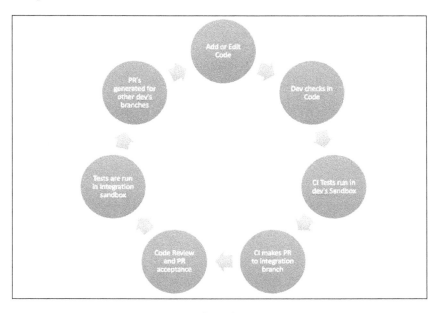

Over the next sprint, they put this process to work. Samantha discovers the process works great, and as the primary Visualforce and JavaScript developer, she almost never runs into any kind of merge conflict. James and Jorge, on the other hand, are both focused on features related to the Account model. Because they're both focused on the same object, their modifications often occur in the same class. Jorge finishes his feature, ensures the tests pass on his feature branch, and creates a pull request for the feature. Accepting the pull request closes out the feature branch and triggers the CI system to run all tests in the integration environment. Unfortunately, unbeknown to him, Samantha removed a field from one of the Visualforce pages, and this is causing a test to fail because that field's contents are no longer available to the controller automatically. When the tests fail, an angry Slackbot notifies the team by mocking the offender mercilessly until they start passing again. Because the entire team is focused on quality, when the tests break, everyone jumps in to help and they quickly identify and fix the problem. When the tests pass in the integration environment and the feature has passed the team's code review, it's time for the CI system to generate pull requests from develop to Samantha, James, and Maddison's open feature branches. For Samantha and Maddison, these pull requests are marked by GitHub as **able to be automatically merged**. Ensuring that their changes are committed to their feature branch, they accept the pull request, knowing it contains passing and reviewed code. Accepting this pull request deploys the newly merged code to their sandboxes, where they can continue to work. James, on the other hand, isn't so lucky. GitHub warns him that this pull request cannot be automatically merged. As it turns out, Maddison set up the CI system with an automatic code style formatter and, because he wasn't following the style guide, he has countless tiny differences throughout one class. Merging this PR takes longer, as James goes through the class looking at all the differences, but in the end, his feature branch is back up-to-date and he can continue working. Later in this sprint, during code review, Maddison rejects one of Samantha's pull requests because the method and variable names don't match the team's naming convention. It's an issue that's quickly addressed, however, and the team continues working on features unhindered by each other's work.

As the release nears, the team merges develop down to master and tags it as a release. After validating the tests pass in production with the new code, it's deployed and another successful release is marked on the calendars.

Making it all work

If you feel as though the above narrative sounds far-fetched or not feasible, I don't blame you. It's not only a massive technological undertaking, but a significant cultural shift for many Salesforce1 platform developers. Unfortunately, the cultural challenges can be immense. Without buy-in from the entire team, this can prove difficult to make worthwhile. Thankfully, the technological challenges, while tedious, are not terribly complex. Let's look at the technical side of things and build out a CI system to meet these needs.

At the core of our setup is the continuous integration system. There are dozens of CI systems, ranging from fully-fledged systems with long histories such as Jenkins, Bamboo, and Team City, to newer, lighter solutions such as CodeShip, Travis.ci, CircleCi, and Drone.io. Most likely, any CI system your company has in use is capable of working with the Salesforce1 platform. The older, more established CI systems will offer more plugins and a richer general ecosystem. However, in the spirit of taking small steps toward our goal, I'm going to use Drone.io for illustration purposes. Drone.io is a light and fast Docker-based CI system that you can host yourself or subscribe to as a service. It has deep integrations with GitHub, and in general, **just works**.

Part of what makes Drone.io so simple is that your test runner is essentially a command line. Inside the Drone.io interface seen here, you'll set up the definition of a test run as a series of command lines:

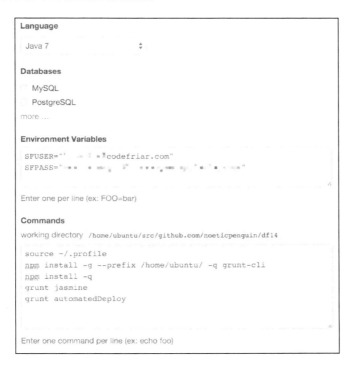

As you can see, the Drone.io interface is pretty Spartan, but it gets the job done nicely. A couple of things to note: first, you need to select Java 7 as the language from the drop-down **Language** tab. This doesn't specify the language your app is written in so much as it identifies the toolset available to you by default. Since `Drone.io` is Docker-based, every test run is done inside a fresh copy of the container, and this language selection box defines the default toolset for the container. Java 7 gives us access to the Java ecosystems including tools such as ANT, which we'll use to run tests and deploy Salesforce code. Secondly, you'll notice that no database under the **Databases** section is selected. This is a per-project decision, and while our project doesn't need a database outside of Salesforce, your project might, so select as needed. Next, look at the *Environment Variables* section. This allows you to insert secret data such as username and passwords into the environment, without having to commit them to version control. Finally, the **Commands** box allows us to enter in our actual build commands. These are run in order and can be used to establish the environment as well as run our tests and take actions.

Fundamentally, whichever CI tool you choose will work largely the same way. It will check out from version control the latest changes into a fresh testing environment where the tests will be run. In the case of a CI system for Salesforce, there's a small twist—we cannot run our tests outside of Salesforce. Therefore, we'll have to use tools such as Ant to run our tests for us. The Ant migration toolkit, like many Metadata API clients, has a plethora of configuration options. In order to make it easier to use and more maintainable, I recommend using a task runner that lets you develop reusable tasks. There are a number of task runners available including, but not limited to: Ant, Rake, Grunt, and Brunch. Regardless of which one you use, the principles discussed here stand true.

This project uses Grunt, a JavaScript-based task runner that allows us to with wrap sequences of commands and conditional logic into singular commands. These simpler commands are easier to follow and set up at the CI level. In fact, our first few commands actually set up Grunt and its ancillary tools via NPM. NPM is the JavaScript package manager. Because `Drone.io` creates a new testing environment for every build, we need to establish our tool chain every build. NPM is a handy way to ship a single file, for example, `package.json`, with the repository code, and use it to install our toolchain. In this case, our `package.json` lists the dependencies we need for the build to succeed. These are my standard go-to packages for establishing a solid CI environment orchestrated by Grunt:

```
"dependencies": {
"grunt": "~0.4.2",
"grunt-cli": "~0.1.13",
"grunt-contrib-clean": "~0.5.0",
"grunt-contrib-copy": "~0.5.0",
```

```
"grunt-contrib-cssmin": "~0.7.0",
"grunt-contrib-jasmine": "~0.6.1",
"grunt-contrib-less": "~0.9.0",
"grunt-env": "~0.4.1",
"grunt-template-jasmine-istanbul": "~0.3.0",
"load-grunt-tasks": "~0.3.0",
"grunt-ant-sfdc": "~0.2.2",
"grunt-available-tasks": "~0.4.5",
"grunt-contrib-compress": "~0.8.0",
"grunt-prompt": "~1.1.0"
}
```

Running the NPM install commands first installs Grunt and then all the dependencies listed here. It's not until we get to grunt jasmine and grunt automatedDeploy that we get to actually test our code. The jasmine and automatedDeploy grunts are tasks defined in the project's Gruntfile. This configuration file is added to version control and is a portable way to automate complex tasks. Looking at a Gruntfile can be a bit daunting, especially if you're not familiar with Grunt, so let's look at it together and break it down. This is a pretty big file, and to help explain it, I'm going to break it up:

```
module.exports = function(grunt) {
  require('load-grunt-tasks')(grunt, {
    pattern: ['grunt-*', 'which']
  });
  var metadataToDeploy = {
    apexclass: ['*'],
    apexpage: ['*'],
    staticresource: ['*'],
    apextrigger: ['*'],
    apexcomponent: ['*'],
    customfield: [],
    customobject: []
  };
```

This first part of the Gruntfile contains the boilerplate code needed to bootstrap Grunt. In the first few lines, we load a plugin, load-grunt-tasks, which is a handy plugin that will read our package.json file and load all grunt plugins that match the pattern. In this case, the pattern states that we're interested in packages starting with grunt-*. This loads plugins for prompting users for information and calling the Ant migration toolkit to deploy code.

Just after loading our plugins, a hash called `metadataToDeploy` is defined. This hash is used by the Grunt plugin `grunt-ant-sfdc`. The hash defines what is included in the `package.xml` file that the grunt plugin builds and uses for metadata retrieval and deployment. As you can imagine, you can edit this to your liking; just ensure that the metadata types you specify are valid. In the case of this example file, we want all classes, components, pages, triggers and static resources. Adding static resources here allows us to automatically update files in static resources and then upload a fresh zip:

```
grunt.initConfig({
    jasmine: {
      js_app: {
// Include paths for both the local user,
// if we're in dev mode, as well as share mode
        src: [
"resource-bundles/app.resource/resources/tests/**/*.js"],
          options: {
          vendor: [
          'lib/jQuery-2.1.1.min.js',
            'lib/jquery-jasmine.js',
            ],
          specs: [
           'spec/unitTests/jquerySpec.js',
           'spec/unitTests/exampleSpec.js',
           ],
           version: '2.0.0',
           keepRunner: true,
           template: require('grunt-template-jasmine-istanbul'),
           templateOptions: {
           files: '!resource-bundles/jsApp.resource/**',
           coverage: 'bin/coverage/coverage.json',
           report: 'bin/coverage',
           thresholds: {
           lines: 30,
           statements: 20,
             branches: 10,
             functions: 5
             }
             }
           }
         }
       },
```

All of Grunt's tasks are configured in its `initConfig` object. This is nothing more than a JavaScript object with task names as keys. Each task defines its own sub-object, and the keys of those subobjects depend on what plugin you're configuring. For instance, this first key is `jasmine`, and it defines a complex child object. `jasmine` is a JavaScript unit testing framework. The `jasmine` object specifies a child object keyed to `jsApp` that configures the options needed by the `grunt-jasmine` plugin. It's important to understand that the various child objects within a task namespace can be duplicated under a different key. This allows you to define not only a `jasmine:jsApp` namespace, but a `jasmine:myApp` namespace, as well. These namespaces act as configuration sets given to the `jasmine` plugin for execution. For our `jsApp`, we're specifying the location of the source files and the location of test files, as well as a few ancillary options for the code coverage calculator. Each of these options is clearly documented on the `grunt-jasmine` page at npm. With that said, I want to draw your attention to the `thresholds` key of the `templateOptions` object. This allows us to set minimum code coverage requirements that, if not met, will cause the test run to fail. This is our mechanism for enforcing JavaScript code coverage on ourselves. Unlike Apex test coverage, Jasmine let's you set up minimum code coverage requirements not only by line count, but also by statement percentage, branching logic percentage, and the total number of functions covered:

```
copy: {
  deploy: {
    files: [{
      src: 'src/**',
      dest: 'deployTmp/',
    }]
  },
},
```

When Grunt was first introduced, it existed to help JavaScript app developers quickly and efficiently prepare their code for deployment. This led to a number of core plugins for handling things such as copying files and minifying CSS. Eventually, a pattern emerged for defining how these plugins work. Given the copy namespace, *N* number of copy configurations are defined as child objects. In this case, we're defining a single child object named `deploy`. `deploy` has an array of objects, each of which defines one or more files to copy from the `src` folder to the destination folder. Here, we're taking all the files in `src`, including subdirectories (the `**`), and copying them to `deployTmp`. We set this up as a safety measure to ensure that we get the latest version of files stored in static resource bundles:

```
clean: {
  deployTmp: ['deployTmp']
},
```

The copy config results in a file-for-file copy of our `src` directory into `deployTmp`. When we're done with the current deploy, the `deployTmp` directory is cleaned up by deleting it. Like our copy object, this clean object has *N* keys, each of which is an array of files or folders to delete:

```
antdeploy: {
 options: {
   version: '35.0',
   root: 'deployTmp/src/',
   existingPackage: false
   },
   automated: {
     options: {
     useEnv: true,
       serverurl: 'https://login.salesforce.com',
       runAllTests: true
       },
       pkg: metadataToDeploy
   },
   test: {
     options: {
     serverurl: 'https://test.salesforce.com'
     },
    pkg: metadataToDeploy
   },
   prod: {
   options: {
       serverurl: 'https://login.salesforce.com'
     },
    pkg: metadataToDeploy
   },
    jsApp: {
    options: {
     user: '',
     pass: '',
     token: '',
     serverurl: 'https://test.salesforce.com'
     },
     pkg: {
       staticresources: [
       'jasmine'
     ]
     }
   }
 },
```

Here's the meat of our grunt config. The `AntDeploy` object defines the environments and options needed to run tests and deploy code from the CI system or our local machines. We can again specify *N* number of child objects, and in the case of the `antdeploy` object, there are three kinds: `options`, `app`, and `environment definitions`. The `options` object specifies which version of the metadata API to use, where our metadata lives, and whether or not we want the plugin to autogenerate `package.xml` for us. `automated`, `test`, and `prod` are all environment definitions. Their options objects override the standard `options` object. For example, the `prod` object defines an additional option of the URL and specifies that the `package.xml` file is to be automatically generated from our `metadataToDeploy` hash. Likewise, the `test` object specifies a different `serverUrl` but still asks the `grunt` plugin to automatically generate `package.xml`.

The `automatedDeploy` object specifies two additional keys: `runAllTests` and `useEnv`. `useEnv` directs the plugin to look to the system's environment variables for configuration options. This allows us to systematically define the `serverUrl`, user, and pass as environment variables. The `runAllTests` key forces the Ant migration toolkit to execute all tests during the deployment. This is how we run our Apex unit tests. Running an `automatedDeploy` from the CI system returns one of two results: all tests pass and the metadata is deployed, or a failure of one or more tests in which case the code is not deployed. Because our Apex test runner is also our Apex deployment tool, the order of operations matters. If, for instance, we were to deploy the Salesforce metadata before testing our JavaScript code, we would be left with an updated Salesforce org but potentially broken JavaScript tests. For this reason, I always recommend that the automated deploy task be run last. That way, if the JavaScript tests fail, the CI system fails the build:

```
availabletasks: {
  tasks: {}
},
```

Grunt allows us to specify a dizzying array of tasks, and remembering them all can be a challenge. The `Grunt-available-tasks` plugin allows us to set up a task named `tasks` that informs the user of what tasks are available. Its output is a helpful form of documentation and looks like this:

```
Running "availabletasks:tasks" (availabletasks) task
antdeploy         > Run ANT deploy to Salesforce (automated|test|prod|jsApp)
antdescribe       > Describe all metadata types for an org
antdestroy        > Run ANT destructive changes to Salesforce
antlist           > List metadata for a certain type
antretrieve       > Run ANT retrieve to get metadata from Salesforce (test|prod)
automatedDeploy  => Refreshes resources and deploys to selected env
availabletasks    > List available Grunt tasks & targets.
clean             > Clean files and folders.
compress          > Compress files.
copy              > Copy files.
cssmin            > Minify CSS files
default          => Alias for "jasmine" task.
deploy           => Refreshes resources and deploys to selected env (test|prod)
deployjsApp      => Deploys the jsApp resource to the specified env
env               > Specify an ENV configuration for future tasks in the chain
jasmine           > Run jasmine specs headlessly through PhantomJS.
less              > Compile LESS files to CSS
prompt            > Interactive command line user prompts.
refreshResources => Refresh the staticResource.zip files
tasks            => Alias for "availabletasks" task.

Done, without errors.
```

And here is the code:

```
compress: {
  jsApp: {
    options: {
      mode: 'zip',
      archive: 'src/staticresources/jsApp.resource'
    },
    files: [{
      expand: true,
      cwd: 'resource-bundles/jsApp.resource/',
      src: ['**'],
      dest: ''
    }, ]
  },
},
```

The `compress` object defines tasks that are used to zip up static resource bundle directories into `.resource` files that we can upload as part of the deploy. In this case, we're defining a `jsApp` directory and specifying that it should be zipped up into the `src/staticresources/jsApp.resource` file. Your chosen development tool may store the unzipped resource bundles in a different directory, or you may have more than one static resource you want to deploy. Wiring up the directories and archive names must be done for each static resource file. While tedious to set up, this allows the CI system to automatically generate static resource bundles from version control:

```
deploy: {
  test: {},
  prod: {}
},
```

Grunt's configuration requires custom tasks with options to define those options as child objects. In this case, the `deploy` object specifies two child tasks of `test` and `prod`. This allows us to specify, from the command line, which environment we're deploying to. Functionally, this allows for running tests like this: `grunt deploy test`:

```
antretrieve: {
  options: {
    version: '29.0',
    useEnv: true,
    root: 'rollback/',
    // existingPackage: true,
    maxPoll: '20',
    pollWaitMillis: '10000'
  },
  test: {
  options: {
    serverurl: 'https://test.salesforce.com'
    },
    pkg: metadataToDeploy
  },
  prod: {
  options: {
  serverurl: 'https://login.salesforce.com'
  },
    pkg: metadataToDeploy
  }
},
```

The `antRetrieve` task pulls metadata from the specified org to the local machine. This is handy for establishing rollback deployment sets. In this case, we're setting up the `retrieve` task to download the metadata specified by the `metadataToDeploy` hash to the `rollback/` directory. If, for whatever reason, we need to revert a deploy, we'll have the current snapshot of the org in `/rollback`:

```
prompt: {
  login: {
    options: {
    questions: [{
      config: 'antdeploy.test.options.user',
      type: 'input',
      message: "Enter the Deploy Username: ",
      }, {
        config: 'antdeploy.test.options.pass',
      type: 'password',
      message: "Enter pass (without security token): ",
      }, {
        config: 'antdeploy.test.options.token',
        type: 'password',
        message: "Enter Security Token: ",
      }]
    }
    },
  },
});
```

This is our final child object of the `grunt config` object. It specifies a prompt set, a series of questions that allow for user interaction during a deploy. This is a fallback option used when an `automatedDeploy` is run but no environment variables are specified for user, pass, and security token. In my experience, this is almost always used by individual developers who are wanting to deploy to their own sandboxes without storing their credentials in plaintext.

The `initConfig` object contains the bulk of the configuration for plugins and task options. However, it doesn't actually define tasks. Those are defined at the bottom of the file by calling `grunt.registerTask` and `grunt.registerMultiTask`. For Grunt, a task is a singular, predefined piece of work. A multitask, on the other hand, is a series of tasks run one after another. To the end user, or our CI system, tasks are indistinguishable from multitasks:

```
// Default task.
grunt.registerTask('default', 'jasmine');
```

Every Gruntfile needs to specify a default task. This is what's run if you just execute `grunt` on the command line. In this case, we've specified the `jasmine` task, which is provided by the `grunt-config-jasmine` plugin:

```
grunt.registerTask('refreshResources',
"Refresh the staticResource.zip files", function() {
    grunt.task.run(['compress:jsApp']);
});
```

Here, we define a task to refresh our static resource files by running the `compress:jsApp` task. This is essentially `syntactic sugar` because anywhere we run `refreshResources`, we could just as easily run `compress:jsApp`. However, it makes the entire system easier to follow and maintain. Note that if you ever need to arbitrarily run a task within another task, you can call the `grunt.task.run()` method:

```
grunt.registerMultiTask('deploy', "Refreshes resources and deploys
    to selected env", function() {
    grunt.task.run([
        'refreshResources',
        'copy:deploy',
        'prompt:login',
        'antdeploy:' + this.target,
        'clean:deployTmp'
    ]);
});
```

This is where things start to get interesting. Our first multitask defines what happens when we call `grunt deploy`. In this case, the task will run `refreshResources`, then `copy:deploy`, then `prompt:login`, then `antDeploy` for the chosen target, and finally, clean up the `deployTmp` folder. Effectively, this is an end-to-end deployment task that ensures the deployment is made with updated static resources while prompting the user to input the username, password, and security token. This task uses the `deploygruntConfig` object to define its targets, as we discussed above. Grunt understands that command-line options after a task name are parameters. If those parameters match `initConfig` child objects, the parameter is passed as a target. Since our `initConfig` object for deploy defines `test` and `prod`, if we run grunt `deploy:test`, we'll receive `test` as our target. This allows us to pass the target on from the `deploy` multitask to the `antDeploy` task:

```
grunt.registerTask('automatedDeploy', "Refreshes resources and
    deploys to selected env", function() {
    grunt.task.run([
        'refreshResources',
        'copy:deploy',
```

```
        'antdeploy:automated',
        'clean:deployTmp'
    ]);
});
```

Similar to our first multitask, this one sets up an automated deploy workflow that refreshes static resource bundles, copies the deploy metadata, does the automated deploy with tests, and finally, cleans up the temp folder. Because our automated deployment task relies on environment variables for its username, password, and security token, it's up to the CI system to set those up prior to running:

```
    grunt.registerTask('tasks', ['availabletasks']);
};
```

Our final task is an `alias` task and is here for illustrative purposes. If, for example you wanted to define a task that runs tests, you could define a task named `runTests` that simply called `[automatedDeploy]`. In this example, we're creating an alias `tasks` that runs `availableTasks`.

Now that we've worked through the Gruntfile, let's take another look at how it's used in our CI build configuration:

```
#Environment Setup
npm install -g --prefix /home/ubuntu/ -q grunt-cli
npm install -q
#CI tests
grunt jasmine
grunt automatedDeploy
```

Our CI tool is responsible for giving us a basic environment and checking out the latest version of our code to that environment. That code base includes a `package.json` file, which allows us to easily bootstrap our environment with the rest of our needed dependencies. Our first two lines tell the package manager, NPM, to download and install the `grunt-cli` tool and also all the dependencies specified by the `package.json` file.

Once our environment is set up, we run the JavaScript tests through Jasmine. If all our Jasmine tests pass, then we run all the Salesforce Unit tests. If those tests pass, the deployment completes, and the build completes successfully.

This setup gets us 90% of a fully automated team environment. What we're still missing, however, is the ability to create pull requests automatically. To create pull requests, we'll need to add to our package.json and Gruntfile.js. We're going to include the Github.js API, found here: https://www.npmjs.com/package/github-api. This isn't a native Grunt plugin, but we'll be able to use it with Grunt by including it in package.json like this:

```
"dependencies": {
// … existing dependencies hidden
"grunt-prompt": "~1.1.0",
"github-api": "~0.10.6"
}
```

Because the Github-api module isn't a native Grunt plugin, we'll need to do some boilerplate work at the top of our Gruntfile. Essentially, we'll need to require the module and do some basic configuration. This is what it looks like to include a module directly:

```
Github = require('github-api');
```

Much like our metadataToDeploy hash, we need to create a GitHub object; we'll rely on environment variables to pull sensitive information:

```
var github = new Github({
    username: process.env.GITHUBUSER,
    password: process.env.GITHUBPAT,
    auth: "basic"
});
```

Note the use of process.env.* here. This instructs Grunt to pull the GitHub username and GitHub personal access token from the GITHUBUSER and GITHUBPAT environment variables, respectively. If you've never manually set an environment variable, you can do so on most POSIX compatible machines by running export key=value. For instance, running export GITHUBUSER=codefriar on the command line is how I set my GitHub username for this project. Now that we have a GitHub object set up, we need to set the repository we're going to interact with by creating a repo variable like this:

```
var repo = github.getRepo('AwesomestCo', 'repoNameHere');
```

With these set, we can start to build tasks that use the GitHub API to grab repository information, or in our case, create pull requests. The `Github-api` module does much of its work in an asynchronous fashion. Grunt, however, is by default synchronous. As a result of this, we'll need to do two things. First, we'll wrap `Github-api` methods in a simple wrapper method, and secondly, we'll inform our tasks that these are asynchronous methods. Let's build our wrapper methods first:

```
function callRepoInfo(done) {
  var x = repo.show(function(err, repo) {
    console.log(err, repo);
  });
}

function makePullRequest(done) {
  var pull = {
    title: "Automated PR from " + process.env.USER,
    body: "This PR has been generated by your CI system",
    base: "develop",
    head: process.env.DRONE_BRANCH
  };
  repo.createPullRequest(pull, function(err, pr) {});
}
```

Both of these methods accept a singular callback called `done`. This isn't actually used in the methods themselves, but act as an internal Grunt API that enables it to wait until the asynchronous methods have completed. To use this, we just need to instantiate a new `async` variable in our tasks and send it as the parameter of our wrapper functions. Here are the task definitions for calling these GitHub APIs:

```
grunt.registerTask('repoinfo', function() {
  var done = this.async();
  callRepoInfo(done);
});

grunt.registerTask('genpullrequest', function() {
  var done = this.async();
  makePullRequest(done);
});
```

This is all we need to enable creating pull requests. To actually call the task and create pull requests in response to successful tests runs, we just need to add it to our `Drone.io` build commands like this:

```
source ~/.profile
npm install -g --prefix /home/ubuntu/ -q grunt-cli
npm install -q
grunt jasmine
grunt automatedDeploy
grunt genpullrequest
```

Of course, this depends on your environment having the local branch name available as `DRONE_BRANCH`. This is a `Drone.io`-specific naming convention. If you're using Jenkins, for instance, the branch is contained in the `GIT_BRANCH` environment variable. All the features of the preceding `Gruntfile.js` need to be intelligently edited to meet you and your team's needs.

While this system satisfies the automation of the most common use case—multiple developers or subteams developing independent features with mutual dependencies—it does not handle hotfixes or merge conflicts. Try as we might, there's no way to completely automate these situations safely. Additionally, your team may use Mercurial instead of Git for version control, or Bitbucket instead of GitHub. The CI system described here is battle-tested and hard fought, but it's still specific to decisions teams I have worked with in the past have made. It is a pattern, not a turnkey solution, and I need to urge you to understand it's steps individually before implementing this yourselves. After all, Git is a Swiss Army chainsaw. You can do anything you want or need, but you can also accidently cut off your foot.

Impressionism versus Cubism

Every developer has their own opinions of what beautiful code looks like. Some of us like to leave opening braces on the method or class definition line. Others are convinced it should be on the line below. Inevitably, someone on your team will inadvertently violate the established style guide. There are several ways to unify the style of your team's code and unfortunately, all of them have their tradeoffs. First, there are traditional development tools such as astyle, checkstyle, or stylecop, that reformat code given a style **rule set**. These work well for the languages they're designed for. Unfortunately, Apex isn't one of those languages. Some of them, such as aStyle, can be configured to use Java while scanning Apex code. This provides meaningful corrections most of the time, but can be confused by non-Java annotations such as `@future(callout=true)`. Sadly, I've not come across an Apex-specific formatter outside of a fully-fledged IDE such as Illuminated Cloud.

It's a bit easier on the JavaScript side as JavaScript is JavaScript regardless of Salesforce. There are a number of well-established Grunt plugins for modifying JavaScript code style, such as `grunt-jscs-checker`. This plugin functions as a style *test*, failing the build if style rules are violated. I like this kind of style enforcement as it keeps the developer from committing non-compliant code to develop.

Along the same lines as the `jscs-checker` plugin, you can also use similar plugins against commit messages, ensuring that each is meaningfully annotated with the Trello task number, or Jira ticket ID.

Rather than enforcing these style checks on the CI server, you can also implement them using Git hooks. Git hooks are scripts that are run whenever a commit is made. They come in pre- and post-flavors, allowing you to run hook scripts before or after a commit. Implementing style enforcement as a pre-commit hook means code is style-checked before being committed. However, this kind of pre-commit hook can often frustrate developers trying to commit work-in-progress code at the end of the day. Additionally, because the commit hooks are stored on individual developer's machines, there's always the risk that one version of the hook script will differ from another's machine. For this reason, I tend to do all the stylistic checking in both places! Letting the developers know pre-commit where their style deviates from the standard provides quick feedback. CI-based style checks, on the other hand, are easy to control and apply consistently.

Speaking of Git hooks, they have a host of other uses. One team I worked on used a Git hook to post commit notes to chatter. Each commit would show up as a chatter post on the sprint record, complete with links to GitHub. Another team used a clever pre-commit hook to check for documentation blocks before each method definition. You could even hook up ApexDoc to a commit hook and automatically build and publish class documentation to a GitHub pages branch!

 ApexDoc is an amazing bit of open source software from the Salesforce Foundation and can be found here: `https://github.com/ SalesforceFoundation/ApexDoc`.

Just about anything you can think of with regard to source code can be automated with Git hooks.

Even with style checks like these in place, they're no replacement for consistent code reviews. Code reviews are, to my knowledge, the best and only way you can enforce variable and method naming conventions. Additionally, code reviews help keep the entire team current on what is where and why it's been done that way. For these reasons, I never automate the acceptance of pull requests. They should all be code reviewed, and only then manually accepted.

All for one, and one for all

The goals of quality, consistency, and simplicity are, I am sure, at the forefront of all our minds, regardless of our team size. When the team grows beyond one developer, however, it helps to remove the humans from the equation by automating as much as possible. This frees the developers to focus their creative work on solving problems for the business. At the same time, it establishes a consistent level of testing—not just unit tests for all the languages involved, but also style tests, commit note checks, and code coverage checks. These CI system checks, combined with individual developer sandboxes and version control, produce a process for development that is safe, effective, and efficient. There may be cultural road bumps as the process is established, fine-tuned, and tweaked. However, these bumps inevitably work themselves out as developers learn to respect one another's decisions during code reviews.

Recently, it came to light that a large German car manufacturer had allegedly rigged their diesel engines to report lower levels of NO2 when in a testing scenario. They coded their software to always pass in a testing environment. Herein lies the ultimate problem teams face while developing on any platform, but especially the Salesforce1 platform: CI, automation, and version control strategies are only as good as the tests that drive the decision-making. If you Volkswagen your tests so they execute and report 99% code coverage while containing no assertions, then you cannot possibly make accurate decisions about the functionality, reliability, or security of your code. Enabling teams to work more efficiently on the platform with automation can actually *increase* risk if your tests are shoddy. This is where code reviews shine. Discovering that a test contains no assertions during a code review is an opportunity for learning; discovering a code defect in production can escalate to an all-hands catastrophe.

Most of the problems teams on the platform face are not unique to the platform. However, the platform has unique features that can greatly exacerbate issues when multiple developers are using the same development org. Implemented correctly, both at a process level and a cultural level, the combination of version control, CI, and automation is incredibly potent. It provides a safe and reliable process and cultural framework for the team to efficiently develop on the Salesforce1 platform without overwriting each other's code and blatantly ignoring stylistic guidelines.

Summary

Team development is by far the most exciting and productive kind of development. However, it's not without its problems. Thankfully, technology and time have given us solutions to these problems. In this chapter, we went through traditional team development problems and their solutions and modified the traditional solutions for the Salesforce1 platform.

In our next chapter, we will build on all the previous chapters to establish what I like to think of as best practices.

My Way – A Prescriptive Discussion of Application Development on Salesforce1

This chapter is intentionally different. With the potential exception of the last chapter, I've tried to maintain a tone of discussion rather than prescription. This chapter, in contrast, is intentionally prescriptive, more so than the last. This is how I build applications and write code on the Salesforce1 platform. The techniques and tips described here have been developed and used in both small and massive orgs. This is intended as an in-depth look at some overarching best practices of architecture—how we structure applications—and engineering—how we code applications. Specifically, we are going to focus on:

- Keeping our applications and code simple
- Testing meaningful things well
- Naming things intuitively
- Auto-documenting our code
- Writing maintainable code

Keep it simple

Of all the things I've learned about software development, the single most important one is to *keep things simple*. It's often technologically fun to craft more complex solutions, especially when learning new technology stacks. I promise, however, the more complex the solution, the harder it is to debug when it fails. Because code is only one option for creating logic on the platform, maintaining simplicity not only means keeping code simple, but also not using code unless we need to. Knowing where to look for implemented logic can be anything but simple. The solution, however, is as maddeningly simple as it is difficult—*always develop declaratively, falling back to code only as a last resort.* Application developers cannot just be code-warriors, but instead must be knowledgeable and comfortable with the vast array of declarative tools provided by Salesforce. Additionally, we must keep up with the new improvements and features each of the yearly releases bring three times a year. To be clear, I don't mean to imply that we should refactor vast amounts of existing code into process builder processes or visual workflows. That's just not practical. However, when a feature such as process builder is released, we should embrace and use that feature rather than writing more code. Code, however, is where we can have the clearest, cleanest impact by keeping things simple.

Chanting the mantra keep it simple doesn't automatically make our code simple. As time goes on, our code inevitably, it seems, gets more complex. Furthermore, because no two orgs share the same complex business requirements, no two orgs are complex in the same way. While it's possible to derive and state guidelines for complexity, they've always felt too nebulous to act on. I've found it's more meaningful to set goals for more tangible things than complexity. For instance, one classic measure of complexity is the Cyclomatic complexity metric, essentially a count of the logical paths a method contains. Traditionally, Cyclomatic complexity is calculated by one of a family of algorithms as part of a static code analysis. Tools such as SonarQube, Checkstyle, and findBugs can inspect code for its Cyclomatic complexity after it's written. Some editors, such as IDEA's Intelli-j, even offer in-editor calculation of such metrics. Sadly, all these are Java-focused, and while they work, they often don't understand Apex-specific changes to the general Java language. Apex's use of List, Set, and Map data structures, for instance, tend to confuse Java static analysis tools. Just because these tools do not operate perfectly in Apex doesn't mean we have to abandon them or the ideas that underpin them. In fact, while not as automatic as static analysis tools, we have another way of inspecting complexity at a quantifiable level: code reviews. With that in mind, let's identify some quantifiable marks of complexity. These are written in the form of questions to be asked during code review. They are, by design, controversial and aspirational. If followed through, they will result in simpler, more maintainable code.

Code reviews – pointed questions for Apex code review

Let's get started with the following set of questions:

- Does this unit of code have more than four `if` statements?

  Methods with more than four `if` statements (`if()`, `else if()`, `else()`) pose a number of related problems. First, due to the verbosity of Apex, numerous `if` statements will necessarily mean longer methods. Second, because each statement creates another logical path through the method, each also represents at least one additional test case to be written. The fewer the number of logical paths through your code, the simpler it is to understand, test, and refactor. Unfortunately, sometimes the business logic we are calculating requires a number of conditionals. For instance, calculating tax for goods sold needs to know the category of product, the buyer's tax exempt status, the price, and the location it was sold. That's easily four or more `if` statements. Look at this example:

  ```
  public Double calculateTax(Id goodsSold, Account buyer){
    if(buyer.tax_exempt__c) {
      if(buyer.shippingState_taxed == true){
        if(goodsSold.price__c >= TAX_THRESHHOLD_LIMIT){
          return .85 * goodsSold.price__c;
        } else {
          return 0;
        }
      }
    } else {
      if(buyer.shippingState_taxed == true){
        if(goodsSold.price__c >= TAX_THRESHHOLD_LIMIT){
          return .85 * goodsSold.price__c;
        } else {
          return 0;
        }
      }
    }
  }
  ```

As it turns out, determining the tax rate is related to, but not the same thing, as calculating the tax due. One way to simplify this code and reduce the number of if statements is to build a method on the Account object to determine if the account's shipping address is in a taxable state and if the account is tax exempt or not. Creating a formula field on the account for should_be_taxed allows us to simplify to this:

```
public Double calculateTax(Id goodsSold, Account buyer){
    if(buyer.should_be_taxed &&
goodsSold.price__c >= TAX_THRESHHOLD_LIMIT){
        return 8.5;
    }
}
```

Creating that formula field on Account allows us not only to reduce code length, but also cut down on our branching logic and write this so that it reads easier in English. Other often overlooked methods for reducing if statements are enums and method extrapolation. For instance, you can write methods that extrapolate the complexity of making a decision into its own method and focus the original method on acting on that decision. In our tax calculation method, that might mean creating a method called shouldBeTaxed (account buyer) that returns true or false. Like our formula field, this would let the calculateTax method act on that decision rather than making it and then acting on it. Ultimately, there will be times where a single method has to be complex and host a number of if statements, but these can and should be established as their own methods.

- How many clauses are there in the if/else statements?

  Like the raw number of if statements, this question aims to identify overly-complex if statements. As developers, we sometimes write if statements like this:

```
    if(x == true && y == true && z == false &&
(a == true || b == true)){

    }
```

The problem with `if` statements like this is twofold: first, they're hard to understand, especially when we're not dealing with variables such as x, y, z, a, and b, but full objects with methods and fields. Secondly, these are much harder to debug. Concentrating the decision-making on a single `if` statement reduces the decision tree, but it means that when any one of those conditions is not correct, you'll inevitably end up breaking the conditions out into nested `if` statements and log output until you've identified which condition isn't being met. Like the first question, enums and method extraction can help overcome this type of complexity.

- Do all `if/else` statements capture all possible logical branches? (Does it end in `else` or `else if`?)

  I find I run into this one pretty often. As developers, we tend to code to expectations. For example, I expect a given variable to only have three possible values, so I code an `if()` then an `else if()`, and then a final `else if()` to handle my three possible values. This works fantastically for two years until someone adds a fourth value to the options. Suddenly, the `if` block isn't handling all the options, and unexpected behaviors (bugs) happen. Always including an `else` clause, even if it does nothing more than create a self-improvement case or e-mail the team, at least handles the unexpected situation.

- Do any of these methods accept more than four parameters?

  First, let me state an exception to this rule. Factory methods for producing test data are exempt from this rule. For instance, a factory method for returning an order may require passing in a user, an account, a contact, and an opportunity, as well as… well, you get the idea. Unlike test methods, most "live" methods accept parameters for one of two reasons: direct manipulation of that parameter or making decisions through conditional logic. Limiting each method to no more than four incoming parameters forces developers to extrapolate decision-making into dedicated methods and encourages developers to write short, concise, and tightly-focused data-manipulation methods.

- Are any of these methods longer than 30 lines?

This is easily the most contentious question. Larger methods are inevitably harder to follow and more complex. The primary benefit of keeping your methods short is that they, by necessity, must also be simple. It's very hard to have multiple logic paths in a method that's only 30 lines long. Additionally, this simplifies your testing as well, as a 30-line method with only four parameters is unlikely to need to test a great number of edge cases. So, 30 lines seem concrete and quantifiable enough, but I think this could use some explanation, as not everything makes sense as a `line`. Conditional logic keywords such as `if/else` each count as a line, but I wouldn't count a line with nothing but a { on it. If your teams coding style uses a line return after the method declaration before the {, the { is a freebie line. So, why 30 lines? I admit this is a fairly arbitrary choice, but over the years I've found 30 lines to be the sweet spot. I can normally create or refactor most methods into no more than 30 lines, not counting comments. The key to making this work is to *compose complex logic methods from small, tightly-focused methods.*

- Do any of these classes exceed 300 lines?

Like the line count for methods, this line count is as contentious as it is easy to judge. Software is a bit like thermodynamics. The second law of thermodynamics teaches us that over time, things progress from order to entropy. Over time, code inevitably goes from order to chaos. No one starts off writing massive classes with multiple responsibilities, but over time, they have a tendency to grow that way. Keeping a fixed limit on class length is a guard against just throwing features, methods, and utilities into any given class regardless of what it's responsible for. Account classes are responsible for account logic, not logic for validating an account's shipping address. That's what an `AddressVerificationUtilities` class is for. The reasoning behind a change to how address verification works is different and separate from the logic behind changing other account data, and keeping them separate allows you to change, for instance, the validation of an address without affecting the account overall. Keeping your class sizes fixed is a simple way to ensure you're actually maintaining single responsibility, which in turn helps lower complexity.

- Is it clear from the naming of classes what each is responsible for?

This one is pretty simple and stems from the trenches of Java software development. I remember once reading the class name `AccountDataFactoryFactory` and thinking to myself that I understood all the words in that name, but not the name itself. If our classes are to be singularly focused, we should intuitively name them. I like to accomplish this in two ways. The first is by naming the classes as simply and plainly as possible; the second to prefix classes with a type designation. In my infamous `AccountDataFactoryFactory`, the class existed to dynamically return a factory capable of generating account data. It was a factory class for building factories. Regardless, the name wasn't as intuitive as it could have been. I think a much clearer name in that situation would have been `DynamicAccountDataFactoryGenerator`. The same holds true for our Apex classes. It's good to designate factories as such in their class name, but when we go off script building factories to return factories, we need to spell that out, as well. To that end, I like to preface all my class names with consistent prefixes that identify the functionality of the class. Test classes are thus prefaced with `test_`, factories are prefaced with `fact_`, and so on. The exception to this is any class focused on an `sObject`. In those cases, the `sObject` itself becomes the prefix.

The following are the class types and their prefix:

Class type	Class prefix
Test	Test_
Factory	Fact_
Account	Acct_ or Account_

With these prefixes in place, I can easily rely on my IDE's autocompletion to help narrow down and find the class I'm looking for. There are many variations on this theme, and some development teams I've worked with have ultimately decided to use the `sObject` as the prefix for all classes, arguing that a factory should only handle one `sObject` type. Either way, the idea is to establish a consistent naming scheme for objects.

- Does this code make appropriate use of constants and enums?

Variables are, by their nature, likely to change. Removing variability, whenever we can, inevitably leads to more robust software, if only because there's one less moving part. I like to always look for the use of constants and enums during code reviews to see how the team has used them. The Salesforce1 platform gives us a couple of unique features that can help us adopt constants and enums. One of the most common reasons I've come across for teams not using constants is that the constant value "may change." With the Salesforce1 platform, we can have the best of both worlds: data that is changeable yet held constant during code runtime. Because constants are defined as static final variables on the class, and because Apex allows us to set the definition of a static final variable when it is defined, we can establish constants in code based on a custom setting, or custom metadata that looks something like this:

```
Public static final string BASE_URL = appSettings.get('base_url');
```

This of course assumes we have a class named `appSettings` with a static method `.get()` that returns a value from a custom setting or custom metadata. Here, we get all the benefits of a constant during execution while still being able to change values without code deployment.

- Are there any uses of `Test.IsRunningTest()` in the code?

  This isn't necessarily a code smell or something I'd fail a code review over. It is, however, something that is not generally needed anymore. With our ability to provide `httpCalloutMocks` for callouts, the biggest reason for variant logic based on execution context has gone away. Code reviews are an excellent way of identifying this kind of tech-debt and, if you've set up mock factories, take a few minutes to fix it. At the very least, file a ticket or record the presence of `test.isRunningTest()` so it can be taken care of in the future.

- Do the tests all contain at least one assert method?

  This one I will fail a code review on. Tests without asserts are liabilities, not tests. The number of required asserts is up to your team, but every test method should call at least one assert method. I prefer more assertions and would recommend at least two: one to assert your test data was set up as you intended, and a second to prove the code works as intended (or not, in the case of a negative test). Unit tests are there to help your team in the long run, and tests without asserts accomplish none of those goals. Make sure every test has active, intelligent assert methods! What do I mean by *intelligent*? You'll know unintelligent when you see it; it'll be about as useful as this assertion:

```
System.assert(true);
```

- Are any of the tests annotated `@isTest(SeeAllData=true)`?

  This is almost an automatic code review fail. There are times when `SeeAllData=true` is required. However, as the platform continues to evolve, the need for this annotation becomes increasingly rare. And 90% of the time I find this annotation in use, it's due to one of three things. 1: the class was last updated several years ago, 2: the developer didn't know any better, or 3: the developer knew better, but didn't want to refactor. Only about 10% of the time do I find a test that actually still requires the annotation. One of the most common use cases for this annotation used to be pricebooks. Tests that dealt with pricebooks used to require `@seeAllData=true`, but ever since Summer 2014, we've been able to use `Test.getStandardPricebookId();`. Unless you're testing things such as approval processes, this annotation is a code smell and should be refactored away.

- How many objects do the Visualforce controllers instantiate?

  A Visualforce controller should instantiate a single object. This forces you to create and adhere to a wrapper object. Your wrapper object can thus be independently unit tested. Your controller's unit tests should create and manipulate the wrapper object extensively and with as many different users, roles, profiles, and permission set combinations. This wrapper will contain all the objects and values that the Visualforce page relies on, and its creation is deeply dependent on the access permissions to that data. Testing with different users, roles, permissions, and permissions sets ensures that your Visualforce page works when the user does, or does not, have access to the data. Not only does this practice simplify writing the Visualforce code and simplify the Apex controllers, it makes it much easier to deal with multiple object types on the same page, especially if you're interacting with them via JavaScript.

- Is this code DRY?

  It may seem unintuitive at first, but asking if the code in question adheres to the DRY principle (Don't Repeat Yourself) is a powerful way to identify and squash complexity. If the code in question repeats itself or the functionality of another method, you've not only doubled your testing workload, but have set up a situation where any bug fixes or enhancements have to be duplicated, as well, if you remember. DRY helps you know where to refactor code out into a shared method or class. This question may be the most important for squashing complexity because the simplest way to reduce complexity in any software project is to remove code. Identifying and eliminating duplicate code helps, if for no other reason, by eliminating code. Non-existent code is the least likely to have bugs.

Remember, too, that functionality may be duplicated not in code, but declaratively. If a piece of code fired by a trigger can now be replaced, or is replaced in other circumstances by a process builder process, then the code isn't DRY. Refactoring these situations where workflow rules, validation rules, and processes duplicate decision-making or data manipulation methods means identifying which solution is more in line with the platform's design principles. That may very well mean deleting code in favor of a process or replacing a trigger with a validation rule. As developers, we must remember that mastering the platform means using the right tool for the job, especially when that tool is not code.

I've said it before, and I'll say it again—tests help you

At the risk of beating a dead horse, I want to again call out unit testing. Salesforce doesn't require unit tests because a Salesforce executive got a bee in his bonnet about platform stability. Tests exist to help you properly architect, engineer, document, and refactor your code. They help you architect your code to handle bulk data situations, complex object interactions, and integrations with third parties. By modeling real-life situations in tests, you know just how the code will actually work. Likewise, unit tests help you engineer your code line-by-line to meet security, data access, and governor requirements. If you find that you cannot easily test something, then you are likely fighting the platform rather than leveraging it. If a design or class is hard to test, take a long, hard look at what your end goal is and how the platform's other tools may help you create this with greater ease. Lastly, tests help document the use cases, failure states, and exceptions you had in mind when it was developed. This is an invaluable tool for onboarding new team members. However, these tests as documentation will really shine when you start to refactor your code. Knowing what it *does right now*, before you start, frees you to refactor with abandon. You'll always know when your refactored work is ready to go, as the existing tests will pass. This is especially important when refactoring to clean up technical debt.

If I've convinced you that unit tests are a good thing, the inevitable question I always get is what should I test? Even after a dedicated chapter on unit tests, there are undoubtedly questions specific to your org, your business, and your industry sector that come to mind. For instance, much of my experience has been with the sales and marketing clouds. Your team may only be responsible for the service cloud, or perhaps you're using the sales cloud in a non-traditional market space such as Software-as-a-Service. The thing is, "what to test" isn't a question with a useful answer. Arguably, the answer is "everything" — or test as much as your company will let you.

Perhaps a better question is where should I start? The answer to that is always a judgment call, and relative to the org. Whenever I inherit an org, I look for a few things that usually end up being, well, areas for growth. The three biggest ones are: the oldest code—by API version—code written by third-party contractors, and finally, code that drives business decisions.

Old code is easy to spot and may be just fine, but the older it gets, the more likely there's a better, faster, stronger, and so on, way of solving that problem. Technical debt, sadly, is often delivered with each new release. Fortunately, if there are well-written tests already, refactoring is easier. On the flipside, I've found that old code is much more likely to have bad tests, or no real tests at all. Here is where the `i++` tests of yore come home to roost. Rather than writing useful tests, old code may attempt to inflate the coverage by simply massing a great number of additive statements (this no longer works by the way). Fixing bad tests is burdensome but will help you in the end.

Looking for code developed by third party contractors is a bit more difficult. Often, the circumstances of their contract demand quick solutions without an adequate "ramp-up" time in the org. As a result, there may be inadvertent code duplication going on. Unfortunately, this is also where I find the majority of tests that have no assertions in them. Sometimes, they'll just be commented out, on the belief that once-proven working assertions can only impede deployment to production. If that's the case, just uncomment the assertions. Even if they aren't there, the tests are usually written out enough to exercise the code. Put in intelligent assertions and bring the tests up to speed. Then, and only then, should you consider refactoring that code.

Finally, talk to the business stakeholders and ask what reports they read and what data helps them make business decisions. Writing tests for business crucial calculations can change the bottom line for a company. At the least, you'll have evidence to suggest such calculations are done correctly. But you may also find, as I once did, that a company had been making opportunity discounts available based on an inaccurate calculation of the opportunity's total value, which led to discounts triple what they were supposed to be. If you ask three people at most companies what their top three business calculations were, you'll likely get five different answers. That's why these are the hardest parts of any system to ferret out. But when you do find them, test them vigorously.

Regardless of where you start, just make sure you start testing. Technical debt accrued through bad or too-little testing is beyond frustrating. Remember, someday, someone else will inherit your code and your tests. And that person may not only have your address, name, and phone number, but rage issues set off by badly-written or non-existent tests.

Make tools, and compose applications

With the advent of Invocable actions, this has become one of my main architecture goals for all projects. Using Invocable actions, you can create libraries of tools that process builder can compose into functional data manipulation apps. So, when I say create tools, I mean build decision-making methods and data manipulation methods, but leave the two of them separate. This allows you to not only utilize the code in Apex, but to expose additional actions to the process builder and flows. Exposing functionality to the declarative development side of the platform empowers your admins and your development team alike to rapidly make alterations to business logic without having to deploy code. There's an intellectual cost to this method of development. Building methods that manipulate data in clear, predictable ways means your org swells with lots of methods. While numerous, they become a private API specific to your org that can be composed into bigger methods and applications. Build the APIs first, then compose those methods via process builder, flows, or Apex to establish the complex business logic.

I find that some developers find this intimidating and threatening. After all, building libraries of code that non-coders can utilize through declarative tools may seem like giving the keys to the kingdom away. But no amount of exposed Apex functionality used in processes or flows will ever replace the raw speed and flexibility of coding a solution. Exposing these kinds of data-manipulation methods for declarative development only helps the business move faster, while freeing us to do new and innovative things that only code can do.

Work as a team

It's possible you work for a very small, highly profitable enterprise company that is using Salesforce as a platform for business software. It's more likely, however, that you're part of a team of developers working on the platform for your large to enterprise-sized business. If you truly work alone, then this section is more about what to look for in a company when evaluating a job offer. On the other hand, if you work on a team.

Finding new teammates is a daunting challenge. It's likely an internal recruiter (or increasingly likely a software program) has sifted through countless résumés looking for keywords such as Force.com or Visualforce. In striving to find the subjective best of that bunch, the résumés are given over to the hiring manager who chuckles over them before his or her first cup of coffee, and determines through some internal calculus who to interview. I think it's safe to say we've all gone through this process once or twice. The process, however, is inherently broken. People are more complex than keywords and numbers on a sheet of paper (have you ever noticed that everyone inevitably prints out résumés?) Résumés can't capture a person's experience, and an hour-long interview spread across numerous groups of people can't do the person justice or capture experience either. Instead of bringing the candidates into a room and having them write a Visualforce page to display a Fibonacci sequence backwards from its 100th character or whatever your company's standard software test is, ask them to do a project with you.

When I say do a project, I don't mean come in for an hour and work through a mostly completed trigger or some unit tests for code the candidate has never seen. I mean take a well-defined piece of actual work from the backlog and ask the candidate to do that work, with you, over a set period of hours. Additionally, pay them for their work. It doesn't have to be a huge sum of money, but it helps everyone to understand that they're doing real work, for a real company, not just fizz-buzzing their way through an interview. Give them autonomy over the project's architecture and engineering in accordance with the job level you're hiring at. An architect should be able to fully envision the solution and interactions all the way down to writing the methods. A junior developer, on the other hand, should probably be given more guidance.

Working a project with a candidate helps everyone feel out the culture, the expectations, and the style of both the existing team and the candidate. You'll learn how he or she writes tests, how quickly he or she picks up your org's API, and whether or not he or she pairs well with other teammates. It may be after working on the project that the candidate says, "No thanks, I don't want to work in this industry." It is equally likely that after working the project, you say I really liked the candidate, but we need a more advanced developer for this role. Either way, both parties have much more information before making their decisions. In order for this to work, however, it has to meet two criteria. First, it has to fulfill a real business need for the team, with no projects pulled from thin air. Pull something from your backlog and work it with the same processes you always do, especially code reviews. Secondly, your team cannot simply dictate to the candidate what to do. You're presumably looking to hire a peer, not a mindless drone. Even if the candidate ends up making a mistake, let them make that mistake and teach them the better way. Doing so highlights how a candidate accepts technical correction, even before the code review.

Finding new teammates is almost a purely subjective exercise. Feelings matter and should be taken into account. However, don't judge candidates too harshly on things such as style and naming conventions. They are undoubtedly indoctrinated to their existing employer's style and naming conventions. Be generous and charitable for things that can be taught.

At times, you may find yourself looking to hire not just a new team member but an entire team. Perhaps you're the code-speaking admin of a medium-sized company with no headcount for Salesforce developers. In these situations, inevitably management's mind drifts off to the land of unicorns, where staff augmentation consulting firms offer champagne and steak to anyone who'll listen to their pitch. Picking the right partner, however, requires far more diligence than one might assume. A bad doctor can, through action or inaction, cause great bodily harm. Likewise, a bad coding partner can leave your org with a legacy of problems and hurt. Even when following best practices, the nature of the job demands a coding partner's time be split amongst several projects (and clients) at a time. There simply isn't time for such consultants to learn your org's API. It's crucial that you're careful and methodical about whom you partner with.

Some partners will give you sample code or internal style guides their developers follow. Those are good signs, but inadequate. I advocate coworking a project with a potential new member instead of whiteboard tests. Conversely, when looking for a coding partner, I strongly recommend testing them. Paying them to cowork a project is likely not a sensible option; if you're hiring a coding partner, you might not be comfortable enough with code to know right from wrong (and that's OK). Instead of a project, give them a test—not a long one, but a meaningful one. Ask them to deliver **functionality**, but don't specify how it should work. For instance, I like to ask for a trio of triggers. The first trigger needs to do a simple cross-object field update. The second trigger needs to manipulate pricebook entries in two pricebooks. The third trigger needs to ensure it's not accidently run recursively.

The first trigger is a trick. If I'm given a trigger back, the code partner is either unable or unwilling to use platform tools such as cross-object workflow rules or processes to provide the same functionality. The problem with this situation is if you're always responsible for dictating the exact method of implementation, you'll most likely end up in a cycle of tweak, test, tweak, test because you're not a dedicated coder. How you specify functionality may not only be inefficient, but unworkable. This isn't your fault, and when you hire a coding partner, you're not only hiring X number of Apex developers; you're hiring their knowledge, and they should feel comfortable pushing back on your requests if there's a better way to do it.

The second trigger is a zinger. Manipulating pricebooks in triggers is full of potential problems, and is in general a questionable idea to start with. Nevertheless, it provides an excellent way to see how they write tests. Note that I'm simply expecting tests to be returned with these triggers, not asking for them. Testing with pricebooks is hard, and testing with multiple pricebooks is even harder. To do so in the context of a trigger complicates matters one step further. Looking at how they write and then test a trigger that manipulates pricebooks shows you if they're current on platform technologies (if they use `@isTest(SeeAllData=true)` then they're not current), the patterns of tests they use, and the number and types of assertions they're using. The tests for this trigger are almost always the determining factor I use when helping others determine who to hire as a code partner. If the tests are well done and were returned without being explicitly asked for, the code-partner gets my blessing.

Lastly, the third trigger exposes the partner's ability to understand and prevent recursive updates to records. The pattern for avoiding this is well-documented and easy to implement. If the trigger utilizes a static Boolean variable to determine if it's already run once, it gets a pass. If the trigger(s) utilize a trigger framework that handles recursion prevention without a framework being specified, they get a glowing review.

Regardless of the contents of your test, give one to potential code partners. Ask them to do their work in a developer edition. Make the test as open-ended as you can, but with clear goals of what you want to see. You want push back and questions from them before they start. When they're done, get their results peer-reviewed on the Salesforce Success Community website, the StackExchange website, or the developer forums. Developers in all three places will gladly let you know what they think of the code you were given. Better yet, go to a local developer meetup group, and have the code peer-reviewed there. You'll be able to ask questions in real time and gather many opinions.

Level up

In ages past, young men would be apprenticed out to a master tradesman. After a period of apprenticeship, they would graduate to a journeyman and after years had passed, the journeyman was recognized as a master of their trade. As a master, it was understood that they would take on and train a new apprentice. Although our training mechanisms have evolved from adolescents learning a trade in the master's house to universities and internships, we still periodically evaluate each other's skills. Whether it's an end of course test, or an annual review, our culture presumes a progression from apprentices to journeymen to masters.

The key to this system is learning to mentor others while being mentored yourself. I don't mean a casual, learn-from-the-old-dude-with-the-three-foot-beard-while-you-work type of mentoring. I mean structured mentorship, with dedicated time on a regular basis to ask questions, banter about ideas, and most importantly, review code. I think we all benefit when we have people we look up to as mentors. Finding and spending time with them daily or weekly helps us grow not only in technical knowledge, but soft skill, as well. The benefits of being mentored are pretty well-documented, and not really in the scope of this book. So, why bring it up?

I bring it up because I'm willing to bet you'll rarely be the least knowledgeable developer in the room. The converse is equally true. I doubt you're often the most knowledgeable developer in the room. Salesforce is such a vast ecosystem that it's likely you're a specialist, even if by accident. Your companies use all of Salesforce's offerings, but it's likely your team is focused on one cloud or another. As a result of this, you likely know more about the cloud your team works with than someone working with a different cloud. You may both be Apex developers writing code, but the way you utilize batch processes or queueable Apex is likely very different. In fact, your experience and knowledge are unique. Sharing your experience as a mentor, blogger, or user group speaker reinforces your knowledge and helps you master the platform.

How does teaching and mentoring help you master the platform? Easy. Science tells us that we're far more likely to remember and use what we teach others because when we're teaching others, we tend to make mistakes. We'll jump in with confidence that we've seen this problem before, or we've done something similar recently. Inevitably, however, we'll get the syntax just a bit off or forget a crucial step. In the process of teaching, we reiterate what we've learned not only by sharing, but by making mistakes and reinforcing the aspects we previously forgot. Additionally, teaching in a mentorship scenario means that we often get to start these kinds of conversations by discussing what the other person has already tried. In other words, we often get to start by discussing what's *wrong* before diving into the proper way of doing things.

There's a YouTube channel called Veritasium whose author, Derek Muller, is a master at demonstrating this. His videos focus on teaching average YouTube viewers basic physics. His PhD work at the University of Sydney demonstrated that traditional expository teaching — watching a video that simply and clearly explained basic principles of physics has a negligible effect on test scores. More importantly, Derek demonstrated that an alternative style of videos based in dialog were far more effective, almost doubling the test scores of viewers. His effective videos first discussed the principle and demonstrated the common beliefs around it. Then, the videos broke down the reasons these beliefs were wrong based on misconceptions or inaccurate science. Only after having walked viewers through what was likely their own original understanding of the situation and breaking it down would the videos explain the real science behind the principle being discussed. This dialogue-based approach is the tool we wield during mentorship. Having to rationally discuss the misconceptions of others in order to convince or teach others how to do it properly cements the principles for mentor and mentee alike.

Teaching others through mentorship can be a heady thing. Don't seek out mentees unless you yourself have a mentor. We need to be taught in order to teach. Having a mentor and being a mentor can help you master the Salesforce platform by providing you with both the opportunity to learn and to teach — to have our misconceptions discussed and overcome, even as we help others do the same. Learning the ins and outs of bulk Apex, unit testing, or any of the Salesforce1 platform technologies best comes through mentoring relationships.

So, how do you find a mentor? If you're looking for a job, find one where the team has members who are willing to mentor you. Ask how you can mentor them. Be determined and confident in your ability to both to be mentored and mentor others. Discuss what mentorship means to a given individual before you start. If you can't find mentorship at work, check out the Salesforce user and developer community groups; look on the left-hand side for all user groups by region to find user groups near you here: `https://success.salesforce.com/featuredGroups`. Work with others to start one up if there isn't already one near you. But don't stop at finding a mentor; find someone you can mentor, as well. If you're the newest person to the platform or the only one in your company, again look to the community groups. Volunteer to speak on a topic or to lead a discussion; find people with questions and issues and work with them to find solutions.

Model your data

I've seen countless orgs where objects and fields have been created just because someone said hey, can we have a field for X? This can lead to a number of problems, ranging from data skew to terribly slow code. Thankfully, a little forethought can prevent this. Data modeling can be hard to do, especially if you're struggling with conflicting stakeholders and their understandings of the platform. I sometimes find it helpful to take a page from consulting and ask the stakeholders to collaboratively answer three questions. First, ask what is the clearest, most succinct statement of the problem. Secondly, ask what is the clearest, most succinct statement of the ideal solution. Lastly, ask if the stakeholders have any ideas on implementing the ideal solution. These questions need to be answered by the stakeholders, but they need to know going in that you're not just going to adopt the first solution they come up with. Oftentimes, adding a field to an object is no big deal. However, changing what field holds a key value, or replacing a relationship with a junction object, poses immediate risk to all declaratively developed functionality and all code, as well as reports and dashboards. While you'll be able to easily identify the pieces as they break in your sandbox (you are doing this in your sandbox, right?), you'll need to be able to count the cost ahead of time. Identifying ballpark figures for how long it will take you to accomplish the addition, or modification, of a field or object not only demonstrates mastery of the system to management, it helps keep you from having to work long hours. Being able to tell manager Mark that this will take either three days, or three weeks, for example, helps everyone understand the magnitude of the problem before you start. It sets proper expectations for workload, because you can either refactor this relationship into a junction object, migrate all the data and deploy it over the next two weeks, or implement the requested feature X. Not being able to give such estimates leads to feature X and the junction object being due at the same time.

In order to develop the ability to confidently alter the system at an object-level, we have to architect it. So, what's the difference between engineering and architecture here? Simple: architects are responsible for designing and documenting systems, whereas engineers are responsible for building the system. Ideally, there is a good deal of interplay between the architects and engineers. The best teams I've worked on have had many engineers who've collaborated with the architect. The key here isn't who's writing what code, but who's responsible for providing the blueprints of the system to the engineers. Without that blueprint documentation there's no 10, 000 foot overview demonstrating the relationships between objects. This is absolutely essential for remotely accurate estimates of object-level refactoring jobs.

Like editors and operating systems, many wars have been fought online over object documentation tools. Put simply, pick one and use it. I've seen everything from high-resolution pictures of whiteboards to PowerPoint files full of painstakingly arranged boxes, arrows, and text. In a pinch, even a collection of screenshots from the schema builder are useful. Until recently, I had yet to discover a data modeling and object documentation tool I truly loved; they all feel entirely too manual and frustratingly slow. Recently, however, I came across an interesting project from fellow MVP Andrew Fawcett. In 2013, he released a native platform application for inspecting and calculating UML drawings of your org (`http://andyinthecloud.com/2014/03/17/going-native-with-the-apex-uml-tool-and-tooling-api/`). His tool, the Apex UML Tool, has a few benefits over traditional tools. First, it's able to generate true UML drawings showing not only objects and relationships, but object methods, as well. Secondly, it actually generates these diagrams from your existing code. Don't already have architecture diagrams for your org? This tool will generate them for you! I encourage you to give it a try, especially if you don't already have diagrams demonstrating objects, their relationships, and fields.

Using these architecture diagrams, you can rapidly identify what objects might be affected by a proposed change. Even more importantly, they allow you to ask engineering questions about the proposed change. Does the proposed solution nest objects more than five levels deep? If so, you can't always assume one query will be able to capture all the data. Does the architecture complicate reporting to the point where Apex will be required to meaningfully determine business critical information? Finally, these types of documents are fantastic for helping you and your team discuss, adopt, or rule out the stakeholders' proposed solutions. For instance, tracking a client's reception of an e-mail document *could be* solved by an account record checkbox, but sending a new document every week would soon run you out of custom fields.

Having the ability to look at an architectural diagram and know in a flash that you could create the account e-mail delivery tracking object as a child of the account helps to not only provide the ideal solution for the stakeholders, but the ideal solution for the org overall.

In order to evaluate the potential change, the entire team needs to be on the same page for relationship types and junction objects. I've heard arguments for biasing towards lookup relationships, and I've heard arguments for biasing towards master-detail relationships. I tend to ask myself whether or not the child object provides meaningful data outside of its relationship to its parent object. If the answer is yes, I bias towards using a lookup relationship; otherwise, I bias towards master-detail relationships. In a way, this is for ease-of-use as master-detail child records are automatically deleted when the master record is deleted.

There are times, however, where that rubric fails, notably the case of the many-to-many relationship. Classically demonstrated by orders and products, we model the understanding that an order contains between one and N products and that each product can be sold on multiple orders. Defining the relationship between order and product requires a many-to-many relationship. Thankfully, Salesforce provides one and only one way of building a many-to-many relationship: junction objects. A junction object models records that are the child record of two master records. Defining a junction object is actually pretty trivial; create an object and order _m2m_product with two master-detail relationships. In the case of our example, you'd create one master-detail relationship to the order and a second to the product. Because they are both master-detail, we must populate both relationships in order to save the record. Thus, every order_m2m_product contains a reference to both the order and the product objects.

If you stop and think about it, the way junction objects work is pretty intuitive. What's not immediately obvious is that junction object records aren't limited to just the two references to parent objects. In the case of our order and product example, the junction object may also hold, for instance, a lookup reference to the contact making the order, or the account the order is to ship to. Additionally, the junction object can have notes, attachments, and activities attached. The junction object also becomes the center of query attention. Because we can easily query parent records information with dot notation, it's simpler to query a junction object instead of querying orders and then querying products. Indeed, you can write one query and retrieve order information, including data from the order's parent account record, while also gathering product information. Something a bit like this:

```
SELECT Order__r.Account__r.Name, Order__r.Id, Order__r.
Contact__r.FirstName, Product__r.Id, Product__r.Name, Product__r.
ProductFamily__r.Name FROM Order_m2m_Product WHERE Order__r.
Account__r.Id = 'awesomeId'
```

In the preceding query, we're pulling data not only from our junction object's immediate parents, but the parent's parent record, as well. Additionally, our where clause is built out based on the order's account ID. This would effectively give us all orders and products that a particular account has made. Including a lookup relationship to contact on our junction object would allow us to query for all orders and products ordered by a given person.

The power and utility of junction objects is virtually limitless, but that power comes at a cost. As soon as a junction object is created, the cost for refactoring that data model goes way up. Because of this, I always ask for and document why this relationship between objects must be a many-to-many relationship. Bias away from junction objects and toward master-detail and lookup relationships, and only ever create junction objects where a many-to-many relationship is clearly needed. While this may seem obvious, it's easy to inadvertently generate a junction object simply by adding a second master-detail relationship where a lookup relationship should have been used.

Modeling your data and your class's methods is easily more of an architecture chore than an interesting engineering challenge, yet this kind of documentation is the single best way to prevent accidental junction objects and data skew, not to mention the best possible way to accurately estimate the time-changing the architecture will take.

Using and abusing the platform – hic sunt dracones (here be dragons)

I'm constantly amused and challenged by people who steadfastly believe that X cannot be done in software. Software is, by definition, not necessarily burdened by hard boundaries and limits. Put simply, I believe we can, with dedication and grit, accomplish pretty much anything with software. In this section, I want to present some use cases and code that overcome platform limitations. These use cases and code demonstrate creative and unorthodox uses of platform features. These techniques should not be front line choices for developing solutions. In fact, while these are all technically possible, there are dragons here, questions that require you to carefully consider why you might not want to use techniques like these even though you can. None of these are outright dangerous, but they are not entirely safe either.

Let's start with overcoming platform limitations during testing. If your organization utilizes API integrations calling out from within Salesforce, you'll be faced with testing a method that both a: manipulates existing data, and b: calls out to a third-party service for more information. Sadly, this is one of those situations where testing the solution is harder than the actual solution. In a testing situation, *you should be inserting all the data that your method is going to need*. But making a DML call — insert — will prevent any further HTTP callouts from executing within that Apex context. Even mocked callouts will throw the frustrating `you have uncommitted work pending` error. That means inserting a contact and then making a call out to populate some additional data from a web service just won't work. Thankfully, Salesforce provides a way to bend that rule just a bit, enough to allow us to make DML and hit a webservice, especially if mocked!

Apex gives us two tools that are helpful here. The first is the asynchronous Apex, specifically the `@future` annotation. Inside the context of a test, the `@future` annotation essentially allows you to switch Apex execution contexts. Because of the Apex context switch, governor limits and DML flags are reset. The second tool is the test method `Test.stopTest()`. Among the many tricks `stopTest()` performs is this gem: when you call `Test.stopTest();`, all `@future` methods are *immediately executed*. When combined together, these two tricks give us a way to both insert new data as part of our test and make mocked callouts. This allows us to test code that needs both properly generated test data, as well as information from a mocked callout to properly make decisions. Here's an example:

```
@future
global static void SomeMethodWithACallout(id accountId){
    TestRestClient trc = new TestRestClient();
    id aId;
    try {
        aId = (Id) accountId;
    } catch (Exception e) {
        throw new exception('You fail.');
    }
    Account a = [select id, name, bar from Account where id = :aId];

    //make your callout
    RestClientHTTPMocks fakeResponse =
new RestClientHTTPMocks(200, 'Success', 'Success',
new Map<String,String>());
    System.AssertNotEquals(fakeResponse, null);
    Test.setMock(HttpCalloutMock.class, fakeResponse);
    System.AssertNotEquals(trc, null);
    String result = trc.get('http://www.google.com');
}
```

Here in our code, we've established a `@future` method that makes a mocked callout. Because of its `@future` annotation, its understanding of DML is separate and distinct from the execution context that's inserting the required test data. Additionally, because we're going to call it from with a unit test, we can use `stopTest()` to force its synchronous execution. Given this test helper, we can then construct a test like this:

```
@isTest
static void test_method_one() {

    //If you're not using SmartFactory, you're doing it wrong
    Account account = (Account)
```

```
SmartFactory.createSObject('Account');
    insert account;
    Test.startTest();
    AwesomeClass.SomeMethodWithACallout(account.id);
    Test.StopTest();
}
```

Obviously, you'd want to do more than just call the mock callout method, but this demonstrates how it works. In this test, I'm making use of the `RestClient` we discussed previously. You could modify the `RestClient` class to automatically call internal `@future` methods when `Test.IsRunningTest()` is run. Doing so would allow you to write essentially unmodified best practice tests where you create your test data and execute your unit of code within `startTests()` and `stopTest()`. In hindsight, this may seem obvious and not terribly dangerous. Nevertheless, I've lost track of the number of times I've explained this technique to developers struggling with testing callouts. While it may not seem terribly dangerous, it does essentially bypass an exception condition that would prevent your code from working properly. I use this pattern all the time, but I also caveat its use with the proviso that it's not sanctioned and may stop working at the next release.

While the last one wasn't actually terribly dangerous and only affects testing, this next one is a bit more meta, and because of that, you should take care in understanding the ramifications of it. With the ability to make callouts from inside the Salesforce1 platform, we gain the ability to use virtually any API available. *This includes the Salesforce1 platform APIs*. This is incredibly powerful with virtually limitless uses. You can, for instance, utilize the analytics API to run a report and process the returned results into records that another report uses. Or you can use the analytics API to execute a report, merge it with an Excel template, and e-mail a report complete with pre-established pivot tables and charts to your executive team.

Perhaps more interesting, however, is the ability to invoke the tooling API from within Apex. Amongst its myriad of tricks, the tooling API allows us to query object data and execute anonymous Apex statements. If you've never used a highly dynamic language such as Smalltalk, Ruby, or Python where meta-programming is a common pattern, the ramifications of invoking `execute anonymous` from within Apex may not be immediately clear. `Eval()` is a basic metaprogramming construct that allows developers to have the computer evaluate code generated from a dynamically generated string during runtime. Let's take a step back and talk about how computers interpret our code.

Whether during compile or runtime, the programming language itself is responsible for translating human readable code into something the computer can do. What differs amongst languages is the grammar the human readable code takes.

Meta-programming is a bit of a mind bender, but the essence of it is that instead of writing code to solve one problem, developers write code that solves many problems, or, as I like to think of it, developers write code that writes code on the fly.

The idea behind `Eval()` in languages such as Ruby, Python, and JavaScript is to establish a compiler or interpreter construct that can accept a string of text and then read and interpret it as if it were actually code. If you're not a coder, you may still be waiting for the punch line; what makes this all very important is that, as coders, we can create that string programmatically, mixing in variables for class names, values, and so on. This allows for highly dynamic software that, in effect, is capable of writing itself during execution.

On the Salesforce1 platform, we essentially have two programming languages available to us: Apex and Javascript. Javascript is considered a dynamic language, Apex not so much. In fact, Javascript provides an `Eval()` method whereas Apex, on the other hand, does not. Sadly, however, Javascript is only available within the browser, so we cannot utilize its `Eval()` method for Apex-based API integrations. How, then, can we create a dynamic `Eval()` method for Apex code? Imagine a situation where a legacy computer system is able to nightly spit out a `report` of field information. That field information is needed to properly construct a CSV file whose columns changed nightly. When working on such a problem, we were shown the JEXL string the nightly API report would give us:

```
variable1 eq '1' or AwsomeVar eq '1' or AwesomeSauce eq '1' or
BowTiesAreCool eq '1' or theDoctor eq '1'
```

JEXL, which you can see in all its glory above, is a programming language unto itself. I needed to evaluate the JEXL expressions rendering a `true` or `false`. Using string parsing functions to replace variable names and operands from static maps of data rendered the JEXL into something like this:

```
variable1__c == true || AwsomeVar__c eq == true || AwesomeSauce__c ==
true || BowTiesAreCool__c == true || theDoctor__c == true
```

The problem is that while I can turn that JEXL into Apex code, there's no native way to take and execute that string. If there were a way to wrap that string in an `If()` statement and execute it, we'd be golden. Here is where `Eval()` comes in handy. With `Eval()`, I can pass in that translated string and evaluate it within an if statement. This allows the fields included in the daily Salesforce export to be dynamically determined from the nightly JEXL output. Whenever the legacy team altered their schema, `Eval()` enabled the Salesforce code to adapt its data export accordingly.

So, how do we create an `Eval()` method? Utilizing the tooling API's rest access to (securely) call `ExecuteAnonymous` means we can construct an anonymous code block and have `ExecuteAnonymous` evaluate it just as if we were using the developer console's `ExecuteAnonymous` window. Note that this establishes two requirements for Apex's `Eval()` to work: API access, which means you can easily lock down what users are allowed to access `Eval()` using classes, and setting up a Remote Site in your org, which allows you to call out to your instance of Salesforce (that is, na4.salesforce.com or cs3.salesforce.com). Because Apex is a typed language, our `Eval` methods will need to return a specific type. In my original use case, I wanted to know the `Eval'd` result of a Boolean expression. To do so, I created a new class, `Dynamic`, and used an excellent tooling API wrapper from Andrew Fawcett (`https://github.com/afawcett/apex-toolingapi`) to build the following `Eval()` method:

```
public class Dynamic {
    public class IntentionalException extends Exception{}

    public static boolean eval(String toEval){
        boolean result = false;
        if(!toEval.startsWith('if')) {
            toEval = 'if(' + toEval + ') {throw new Dynamic.Intention
alException(\'true\');} else {throw new Dynamic.IntentionalException(
\'false\');}';
        }
        ToolingAPI x = new ToolingAPI();
        try{
            ToolingAPI.ExecuteAnonymousResult toolingResult =
x.executeAnonymousUnencoded(toEval);
        } catch (IntentionalException ie) {
            result = (ie.getMessage() == 'true') ? True : False;
        }
        return result;
    }
}
```

I'm using an exception so that I can capture and return typed data from the `ExecuteAnonymous` call. That way, our regular code can listen for and catch a particular type of exception, in this case, `IntentionalException` when successful, while still retaining the ability for our anonymously executed code to throw a different kind of exception. Of course, this represents only the Boolean data type, but you could just as easily return JSON serialized representations of records, or even arrays of IDs.

The Eval() is just the start. With the tooling API at our command from within Apex, we can even dynamically generate classes. One of the open source packages I created and maintain is called **Custom Related Lists**, and it allows users to mimic related lists but with the added ability to insert filters. In other words, you can create a related list that excludes inactive contacts or opportunity line items that are backordered. This work is accomplished by using Visualforce as a templating language and the tooling API to write controllers, Visualforce pages, and unit tests.

The user selects the master object whose detail pages this list will display, and the detail object whose records will be displayed on the list. Once selected, the user can select the fields to display, as well as define criteria filters. The wizard is intentionally dynamic; selecting the master object automatically determines which objects relate to it and populates the detail selection list with related objects. Once the user has specified the details, the page controller first saves the record and then generates the controller, test, and Visualforce pages needed:

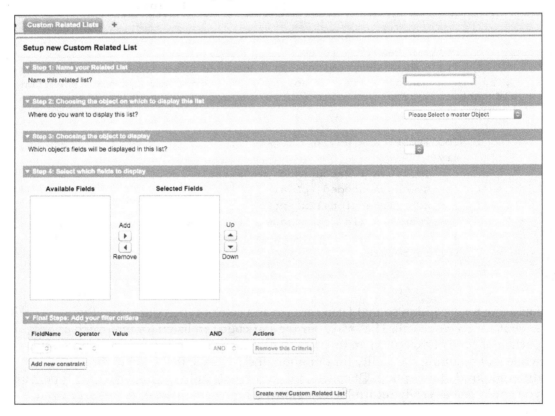

Fundamentally, I'm (ab)using Visualforce as a template system to abstract out the boilerplate bits of Apex and Visualforce necessary to create the related lists. It consists of three Visualforce template files:

- `CRL_MetaGenCtrl`: The controller template
- `CRL_MetaGenPage`: The Visualforce page template
- `CRL_MetaGenTests`: The Apex tests for the controller

Each of these files uses the `CRL_MetaGenCtrl` controller, which is responsible for providing the non-boilerplate bits of code generated from the templates I mentioned above, using a little-known `pageReference` method — `getContents()`. `getContents()` renders the given Visualforce page into a string as if it were requested by a browser.

 Note that in the latest API versions, `getContents()` is treated as a callout.

This allows us to use Visualforce as a templating system. Tied to a custom controller, the templates mentioned above are rendered in Apex through `getContents()` and result in dynamically generated Apex code with the user-selected options merged in. For example, to be included on the detail page of the master object, the Visualforce page that displays the list must extend the standard controller of the master object. The template for the page references a controller extension for the related list, as well as the standard controller, for the master object. Given our example of accounts and contacts, the custom related list page has this page tag:

```
<apex:page standardController="Account" extensions="CRL_conOnAct">
```

Similarly, the CRL_MetaGenCtrl has a method to generate the `startPageTag`, which is used to dynamically specify the standard controller and extensions to the final Visualforce page with standard merge syntax `{!startPageTag}`.

After the custom controller extension, test, and Visualforce page are rendered to strings, the application puts the code in place. Apex code is placed with the tooling API and the Visualforce page is placed with a standard REST call because of how custom related lists uses the tooling API. It's important to note that generating the code will only work in sandboxes and developer orgs. Running the generated code to display a custom related list, however, works in all orgs.

There are, of course, other considerations to keep in mind when doing this kind of out-of-the-box engineering. It would be a pain to regenerate the code and deploy a new change set every time we wanted to adjust what fields are displayed in the list. To prevent that need, the generated code references a custom related list object record upon page load. This allows admins to change the criteria or modify field sets without having to regenerate the code and deploy it. However, this also means that users would have to recreate the record in the production org. To prevent this need, the generated code contains a JSON encoded version of the initial `Related_Lists__c` record. After deployment to production, on the first display of the related list, the code will deserialize the JSON and create the needed record. Keeping your code, even your dynamically generated code, portable makes the entire experience much smoother for the user.

When using Visualforce as a templating system, it's important to consider what you're going to do with the resulting code. To actually take and deploy the code generated by the template, you'll need to ensure your template's page tag specifies a `contentType` of `text/text` like this:

```
<apex:page showHeader="false"
  sidebar="false"
  standardController="Related_List__c"
  extensions="CRL_MetaGeneratorCtrl"
  contentType="text/text"
>
```

Generating code with Visualforce is a neat trick, but it's useless if you can't get it back into your org. To generate and deploy the code, I use this class:

```
public with sharing class CRL_CodeGenerationLib {
private static ToolingAPI tooling = new ToolingAPI();
  @TestVisible private static Map<String, String> pageDetails;

  public static boolean GenerateClass(String body) {
    system.debug('Generating Class');
    ToolingAPI.ApexClass apexClass = new ToolingAPI.ApexClass();
    apexClass.Body = body;
    ToolingAPI.SaveResult sr = tooling.createSObject(apexClass);
    system.debug(sr);

    return true;
  }
```

```
    public static boolean generatePage(String pageName, String body) {
        System.debug('Generating Page');
        String salesforceHost = System.Url.getSalesforceBaseURL().
toExternalForm();
        String url =  salesforceHost + '/services/data/v29.0/sobjects/
ApexPage';
        HttpRequest req = new HttpRequest();

        //Sanitize the input'd page name to strip whitespace and replace
spaces with _'s
        pageName = pageName.trim();
        pageName = pageName.replaceAll(' ', '_');

        pageDetails = new Map<String, String>();
        pageDetails.put('Name', pageName);
        pageDetails.put('Markup', body);
        pageDetails.put('ControllerType', '1');
        pageDetails.put('MasterLabel', pageName);
        pageDetails.put('ApiVersion', '33.0');
        String PagePayload = JSON.serialize(pageDetails);

        req.setMethod('POST');
        req.setEndpoint(url);
        req.setHeader('Content-type', 'application/json');
        req.setHeader('Authorization', 'Bearer ' + UserInfo.
getSessionId());
        req.setBody(PagePayload);

        Http http = new Http();

        HTTPResponse res = http.send(req);
        System.debug('Page Generation Response: ' + res.getBody());

        return true;
    }

}
```

I found it interesting to learn that I could generate a custom Visualforce page simply by posting the page contents to the proper URL. Creating the Apex classes and tests requires the tooling API wrapper I discussed earlier.

Finally, I want to demonstrate how you can use language constructs to solve oddly difficult problems. I was once faced with the need to merge contact information into a block of text outside of a Visualforce page. In fact, I essentially needed to do a mail merge without sending any e-mails before doing some additional processing. Unfortunately, there's no built-in way to do that. Salesforce's Visualforce e-mail template API doesn't give you a "getter" for the merge result. Instead, the normal workflow looks like this:

```
Messaging.SingleEmailMessage mail = new Messaging.
SingleEmailMessage();
    String[] toAddresses = new String[]{'theDoctor@who.com'};
    mail.setToAddresses(toAddresses);
    mail.setUseSignature(this.useSig);
    mail.setSaveAsActivity(this.saveActivity);
    mail.setSenderDisplayName(this.senderDisplayName);
    mail.setTargetObjectId(targetObjectId);
    mail.setTemplateId(templateId);
    Messaging.sendEmail(new Messaging.SingleEmailMessage[] {mail});
```

There's not even a `.merge()` method exposed in Apex. The merging happens as part of `Messaging.sendEmail();`.

I decided to wrap the workaround I found in a reusable class: `MailUtils.cls`. The `MailUtils.cls` offers a single static method: `getMergedTemplateForObjectWith outSending(Id targetObjectId, Id templateId, Boolean useSig, Boolean saveActivity, and String senderDisplayName)`. That takes the work out of this. It returns a map with the following keys:

- `textBody`: Merged text body
- `htmlBody`: Merged HTML version
- `subject`: Subject line of the e-mail

Here's `MailUtils.cls` in its full glory:

```
public class mailUtils {
  public class mailUtilsException extends exception {}

  public Boolean useSig {get; private set;}
  public Boolean saveActivity {get; private set;}
  public String senderDisplayName {get; private set;}

  public mailUtils(Boolean useSig, Boolean saveActivity, String
senderDisplayName){
    this.useSig = usesig;
```

```
        this.saveActivity = saveActivity;
        this.senderDisplayName = senderDisplayName;
    }


    // Derived from:
    // http://salesforce.stackexchange.com/questions/13/using-apex-to-
assemble-html-letterhead-emails/8745#8745
    public Messaging.SingleEmailMessage MergeTemplateWithoutSending(Id
targetObjectId, Id templateId) {
        Messaging.reserveSingleEmailCapacity(1);
        Messaging.SingleEmailMessage mail = new Messaging.
SingleEmailMessage();
        // Intentionally set a bogus email address.
        String[] toAddresses = new String[]{'invalid@emailaddr.es'};
        mail.setToAddresses(toAddresses);
        mail.setUseSignature(this.useSig);
        mail.setSaveAsActivity(this.saveActivity);
        mail.setSenderDisplayName(this.senderDisplayName);
        mail.setTargetObjectId(targetObjectId);
        mail.setTemplateId(templateId);

        // create a save point
        Savepoint sp = Database.setSavepoint();
        // Force the merge of the template.
        Messaging.sendEmail(new Messaging.SingleEmailMessage[] {mail});
        // Force a rollback, and cancel mail send.
        Database.rollback(sp);

        // Return the mail object
        // You can access the merged template, subject, etc. via:
        // String mailTextBody = mail.getPlainTextBody();
        // String mailHtmlBody = mail.getHTMLBody();
        // String mailSubject = mail.getSubject();
        return mail;

    }

    public static Map<String,String> getMergedTemplateForObjectWitho
utSending(Id targetObjectId, Id templateId, Boolean useSig, Boolean
saveActivity, String senderDisplayName) {
        Map<String,String> returnValue = new Map<String,String>();
        mailUtils mu = new mailUtils(useSig, saveActivity,
senderDisplayName);
        Messaging.SingleEmailMessage mail = mu.MergeTemplateWithoutSending
(targetObjectId, templateId);
```

```
        returnValue.put('textBody', mail.getPlainTextBody());
        returnValue.put('htmlBody', mail.getHTMLBody());
        returnValue.put('subject', mail.getSubject());
        return returnValue;
    }

}
```

I draw attention to this use case because of the way it uses a savepoint and rollback to capture the results of the e-mail merge. It exposes the way a DML rollback doesn't roll back the state of a given object. Once the rollback occurs, we have access to a merged `Messaging.SingleEmailMessage` instance. Getting the text body, HTML body, and subject is as simple as calling their getters.

Again, I want to state you should adopt patterns like these after careful consideration of the ramifications. These are incredibly powerful, but unsafe in the wrong hands.

Summary

Here we are at the end of our book. Hopefully, you've learned a bit and enjoyed your time. We've covered a lot during these nine chapters. Indeed, we've discussed quite a lot in just this last chapter. One of the most important things we talked about in this chapter is the idea of leveling up—mentoring and being mentored. One of my favorite aspects of the Salesforce community is the breadth and depth of knowledge freely shared on blogs, in the success community, and in countless other ways. I would be remiss if I didn't highlight some of these resources before our journey ends.

Where to go from here

There are a number of blogs that I follow dedicated to the Salesforce ecosystem. Not every one of these is code-focused, but they've all taught me a number of things. In no particular order, here are a few to get you started:

`http://www.codefriar.com`—OK, shameless plug here; this one is my blog. I mostly talk about Salesforce and mobile development.

`http://www.adminhero.com/`—Brent Downey spends his blog time helping readers understand how to get the most out of your Salesforce org. While Brent doesn't do much with code, his blog is invaluable when it comes to mastering the declarative aspects of the Salesforce ecosystem.

`http://andyinthecloud.com/` — Andrew Fawcett's blog is the gold standard for code-based Salesforce blogs. He's responsible for building a number of free packages like the Declarative Lookup Rollup Summary tool, and the UML chart generation tool I mentioned in the team development chapter. His articles are easy-to-read and packed full of useful information.

`https://www.buttonclickadmin.com/` — Whereas Andrew's blog is the gold standard for coding blogs, Mike Gerholdt is the venerable gold standard for declarative development blogs.

Podcasts

Podcasts are a great way to learn while you are driving to work, or otherwise occupied by a mind-numbingly boring task. There're only a couple I want to highlight here, but they're well worth your time:

`https://itunes.apple.com/us/podcast/code-coverage-salesforce-developer/id880831007?mt=2` — *Code Coverage* is led by two of the smartest and most experienced developers I've ever met. Matt Lacey and Steven Herod spend their podcast time interviewing various people in the Salesforce ecosystem on a wide range of topics. Want to learn more about Trailhead, for example? Check out Episode 21.

`http://thewizardnews.com/wizardcast_home/` — Just as informative, but with a lighter-hearted tone, is the *WizardCast*. Led by two characters known as SalesforceWizard (complete with wizard hat!) and SalesforceYoda, these two will make you laugh, even as you learn all about using flows.

Online help, training, and chat

First, do not pass go, and do not collect $200 — go here: `https://developer.salesforce.com/trailhead`, sign up, and start working though trails. It doesn't matter what your experience with Salesforce development is, go work through Trailhead. If nothing else, it's a great way to highlight your skills on your LinkedIn page! Trailhead is different than other online learning systems because most of the trails require you to log in to a development org and demonstrate your skills, not just answer questions. In other words, you'll learn a skill, say how to write a bulk trigger, and then you'll have to actually build a bulk trigger! Trailhead will then execute tests against your trigger and only if it passes will you get the points and the badge.

Despite the skills you'll pick up going through Trailhead, you're inevitably going to run into an issue or quirk of the platform that you just don't quite understand. When that happens, here are a few resources you can reach out to online.

`https://success.salesforce.com/` — The venerable Success community is home to the largest online community for any platform I've ever discovered. Here, you can ask your questions, no matter how big, small, detailed, or just plain noobish. If you're lucky, your questions will be answered by some of the community's legends such as Steve Molis. Remember to search the archives before posting! It's likely you're not the first person with this problem, and there may already be an answer waiting for you!

Like the Success community, the Salesforce Developer forums are a great place to ask and answer questions related to Salesforce development. While you're more likely to find questions and answers about validation rules and page layouts within the Success community, you're more likely to find detailed questions about Apex collections and HTTP callouts on the Developer forums. This is a great place to get your feet wet answering questions. Do make sure, however, to use the code formatting and hyperlinking buttons to properly set up your code and links.

Code writing developers from any background are likely familiar with StackExchange. What you may not know is that there's a StackExchange specifically for Salesforce: `http://salesforce.stackexchange.com/`. Here, you'll find a tightly moderated question and answer site covering everything from Apex enums to Marketing Cloud AmpScript questions, along with detailed, useful answers. Note, however, that the StackExchange system does not take kindly to questions that simply ask someone else to do your work.

Remember that with any of these three question and answer sites, it's always best to present your formulas, code, or validation rules in their entirety. It's frustrating to try and help only to discover that the problem is clearly in the method you didn't share.

Lastly, there's an old means of real-time communication called Internet Relay Chat, or IRC. IRC has federated server networks that individuals connect to, and rooms that are tied to topics. The community maintains a fairly vibrant room, called #salesforce on the Freenode network. You can join us by visiting: `https://webchat.freenode.net/`. You'll need to supply your own nickname and prove you're human, but if you do that and specify #salesforce for the channels input, you'll soon see messages scrolling across your browser. Feel free to ask questions; we don't bite.

Thanks for reading my book! Feel free to follow me on Twitter at `@codefriar`.

Index

Symbols

@auraEnabled Apex 67
@future annotated methods
  exploring 43, 44
  using 44
@InvocableActions interface 54-57

A

access token
  implementing 120, 121
anonymous Apex
  executing 14, 15
Ant migration toolkit
  about 98, 99
  build.xml file 99-101
Apex
  schedulable classes, scheduling 41, 42
ApexDoc
  about 170
  URL 170
APIs
  integrating, into Salesforce 144, 145
application development
  development tools, identifying 4, 5
  for cloud computing 2
  object-oriented development 6
  with Salesforce1 7
application development, best practices
  application, testing 182, 183
  code, maintaining simple 174
  code reviews 175-182
  data modeling 190-193
  Invocable actions, using 184

level up, by mentoring 187-189
  platform limitations, overcoming 193-204
  teamwork, implementing 184-187
assertions
  about 90
  custom assertion methods, creating 91, 92
Asynchronous Apex
  usage guidelines 48
asynchronous code 33
AuraDocs
  URL 66
Authorization 118
automated solutions, team development
      problems
  code, reviewing 171
  continuous integration system,
      implementing 152-154
  continuous integration system,
      building 155-169
  Git, implementing 150-152
  Git hooks, using 169, 170
  version control, implementing 152-154

B

batchable classes
  Database.AllowsCallouts interface,
      implementing 36-39
  Database.Stateful interface,
      implementing 36-39
  using 33-36
build properties
  about 102
  example 102, 103
built-ins 102

bulk data API
about 123-126
limitations 127
reference link 127
use cases 127, 128
versus standard sObject REST
API 123, 124
bulk safety 22

C

Change Sets
about 109
components, adding 111, 112
cloud computing 2
Component files 63-67
Concurrent Versions System (CVS) 148
Continuous Integration (CI) systems 94
create, read, update, and delete (CRUD) 117
custom API
creating 128-131
data, deleting 134, 135
data, updating 133
records, adding 131-133
request object, creating 136-143
custom assertion methods
creating 91, 92

D

Database.AllowsCallouts interface
implementing 36-39
Database.Stateful interface
implementing 36-39
data manipulation language (DML) 18, 80
debug logs
opening 12-14
reading 12-14
deployment 97
destructiveChanges.xml file 105
developer console, Salesforce
anonymous Apex, executing 14, 15
debug logs, opening 12-14
debug logs, reading 12-14
lightning components, creating 12
lightning components, opening 12
log levels, adjusting 12-14
metadata, creating 8

metadata, opening 8
problems, addressing 15, 16
SOQL queries, running 8, 9
SOSL queries, running 8, 9
unit tests, running 10, 11
using 7

E

external lookups 59
external objects 59
Extract, Transform, and Load (ETL) 116

F

FFLib_ApexMocks
URL 92
Force.com IDE
deploying 106-108

G

Git 150-152
Git hooks
using 170
Grunt
using 156-169

H

hammer 74

I

Illuminated Cloud
about 4
URL 4
indirect lookup 59

L

Lightning App Builder 68-72
Lightning Components
@auraEnabled Apex 67
about 61, 62
Component files 63-67
creating 12
in future 68
opening 12

Lightning Connect
about 58
example use cases 61
limitations 59, 60
Lightning Process Builder
@InvocableActions interface 54-57
about 52, 53
caveats 57
implementing 58
log levels
adjusting 12-14

M

macros 102
managed package code
unit tests, avoiding 77
max loop count API 27
metadata
Change Sets 109-112
creating 8
destructiveChanges.xml file 105
Force.com IDE, deploying 106-108
opening 8
selecting 103, 104
meta-tests 152
mocking 92, 93
modern APIs
evolution 116, 117
multiple triggers
creating 24

N

negative tests 83, 84

O

oAuth 117-119
object-oriented development 6

P

permissions-based tests 84-89
positive tests 82
Postman
URL 118

Q

queueable classes
about 45
testing 47, 48

R

Representational State Transfer
(REST) API
about 117
implementing 122, 123
Revision Control System (RCS) 148

S

Salesforce
APIs, integrating into 144, 145
community groups, URL 189
schedulable classes
about 40
monitoring 41
scheduling, from Apex 41, 42
testing 42, 43
SFDC-trigger-framework
about 25
cautionary note 26
URL 25
using 27-30
Simple Object Access Protocol (SOAP) 116
SOQL queries
running 8, 9
SOSL queries
running 8, 9
Source Code Control System (SCCS) 148
standard platform features
unit tests, avoiding 77
standard sObject REST API
versus bulk data API 123, 124

T

targets 102
team development problems
about 148, 149
automated solutions 150
code, overwriting 149

test-driven development (TDD) 77
Test-Factory
  URL 79
triggers
  bulk safety, implementing 22, 23
  context 18
  example 19-21
  multiple triggers, creating 24
  overview 17
  trigger variables 19

U

unit tests
  avoiding, for managed package code 76, 77
  avoiding, for standard platform features 77
  code, executing 81
  custom data, using 78-80
  negative tests 83, 84
  permissions-based tests 84-89
  positive tests 82
  running 10, 11
  starting 81
  stopping 81
  structuring 78
  tips and tricks 93-95
  usage 77
  writing 74
unit tests, advantages
  bugs, reducing 76
  change cost, reducing 75
  code, documenting 76
  engineering bugs, identifying 75
  functionality, proving 74
  modular code, encouraging 75
  reusable code, encouraging 75

V

Veritasium
  URL 189
Version Control Systems 148

W

Web Service Definition Language
  (WSDL) 116

Thank you for buying
Mastering Application Development
with Force.com

About Packt Publishing

Packt, pronounced 'packed', published its first book, *Mastering phpMyAdmin for Effective MySQL Management*, in April 2004, and subsequently continued to specialize in publishing highly focused books on specific technologies and solutions.

Our books and publications share the experiences of your fellow IT professionals in adapting and customizing today's systems, applications, and frameworks. Our solution-based books give you the knowledge and power to customize the software and technologies you're using to get the job done. Packt books are more specific and less general than the IT books you have seen in the past. Our unique business model allows us to bring you more focused information, giving you more of what you need to know, and less of what you don't.

Packt is a modern yet unique publishing company that focuses on producing quality, cutting-edge books for communities of developers, administrators, and newbies alike. For more information, please visit our website at www.packtpub.com.

About Packt Enterprise

In 2010, Packt launched two new brands, Packt Enterprise and Packt Open Source, in order to continue its focus on specialization. This book is part of the Packt Enterprise brand, home to books published on enterprise software – software created by major vendors, including (but not limited to) IBM, Microsoft, and Oracle, often for use in other corporations. Its titles will offer information relevant to a range of users of this software, including administrators, developers, architects, and end users.

Writing for Packt

We welcome all inquiries from people who are interested in authoring. Book proposals should be sent to author@packtpub.com. If your book idea is still at an early stage and you would like to discuss it first before writing a formal book proposal, then please contact us; one of our commissioning editors will get in touch with you.

We're not just looking for published authors; if you have strong technical skills but no writing experience, our experienced editors can help you develop a writing career, or simply get some additional reward for your expertise.

Learning Force.com Application Development

ISBN: 978-1-78217-279-6   Paperback: 406 pages

Use the Force.com platform to design and develop real-world, cutting-edge cloud applications

1. Design, build, and customize real-world applications on the Force.com platform.

2. Reach out to users through public websites and ensure that your Force.com application becomes popular.

3. Discover the tools that will help you develop and deploy your application.

Force.com Development Blueprints

ISBN: 978-1-78217-245-1   Paperback: 350 pages

Design and develop real-world, cutting-edge cloud applications using the powerful Force.com development framework

1. Create advanced cloud applications using the best Force.com technologies.

2. Bring your cloud application ideas to market faster using the proven Force.com infrastructure.

3. Step-by-step tutorials show you how to quickly develop real-world cloud applications.

Please check **www.PacktPub.com** for information on our titles

Force.com Enterprise Architecture

ISBN: 978-1-78217-299-4   Paperback: 402 pages

Blend industry best practices to architect and deliver packaged Force.com applications that cater to enterprise business needs

1. Build your own application from start to finish, making use of unique tools and platform features.

2. Learn how to use the platform to build a truly integrated, scalable, and robustly engineered application to design, develop, package, and support an application focusing on enterprise-level customer demands.

Learning Apex Programming

ISBN: 978-1-78217-397-7   Paperback: 302 pages

Create business applications using Apex to extend and improve the usefulness of the Salesforce1 Platform

1. Create Apex triggers and classes and build interactive Visualforce pages.

2. Understand best practices and workarounds to platform limitations.

3. Hands-on examples that will help you create business applications using Apex quickly and efficiently.

Please check **www.PacktPub.com** for information on our titles

www.ingramcontent.com/pod-product-compliance
Lightning Source LLC
Chambersburg PA
CBHW060550060326
40690CB00017B/3660